THE ART
OF WAR
ILLUSTRATED

The Art of War Illustrated is a new translation of Sun Tzu's classic text combined with illustrative case studies that provide expert military commentaries on the 13 parts of the original work.

The case studies include battles and campaigns from throughout history and from every part of the world, offering the reader a relevant military context for each aspect of warfare and how that applies to military strategy and tactics.

THE ART
OF WAR
ILLUSTRATED

SUN TZU

TRANSLATED BY JAMES TRAPP

Published by Amber Books Ltd
United House
London N7 9DP
United Kingdom
www.amberbooks.co.uk
Instagram: amberbooksltd
Facebook: www.facebook.com/amberbooks
Twitter: @amberbooks

ISBN: 978-1-78274-701-7

Translator: James Trapp
Project Editor: Michael Spilling
Designer: Zoe Mellors
Picture research: Terry Forshaw

Printed in China

4 6 8 10 9 7 5

PICTURE CREDITS:
Alamy: 25 (Science History Images/Photo Researchers), 35 (Atlaspix), 44 (World History Archive), 81 (Art Collection), 101 (Ian Dagnall Commercial Collection), 102 (Chronicle), 145 (US Army), 157 (Science History Images/Photo Researchers)
Art-Tech: 15
Cody Images: 53, 55
Depositphotos: 89 (Beibaoke)
Getty Images: 67 (Corbis/Peter Turnley), 69 (Corbis/Peter Turnley), 114 (Corbis/Minnesota Historical Society), 146 (Corbis/Tim Page)
Library of Congress: 113, 115, 116
Ukrainian State Archive: 56, 57, 133, 134, 135
US Department of Defense: 42, 43, 117

All maps © Amber Books Ltd

TRADITIONAL CHINESE BOOKBINDING

This book has been produced using traditional Chinese bookbinding techniques, using a method that was developed during the Ming Dynasty (1368–1644) and remained in use until the adoption of Western binding techniques in the early 1900s. In traditional Chinese binding, single sheets of paper are printed on one side only, and each sheet is folded in half, with the printed pages on the outside. The book block is then sandwiched between two boards and sewn together through punched holes close to the cut edges of the folded sheets.

INTRODUCTION

It is an unusual book that was written 2500 years ago in an impenetrable classical language and yet figures on the recommended reading list of the United States Marine Corps. More unusual still for it to be a favourite book of figures so contrasting as General Douglas MacArthur and Mao Zedong (Mao Tse Tung); but Sunzi's 兵法 [*Art of War*] is such a book. Moreover it has discovered a new life outside military circles in the world of modern business management. A simple internet search under '*Art of War* + business strategy' will provide hundreds of sites claiming to offer invaluable commercial insights based on this ancient text.

According to long tradition, 兵法 was written by Sun Wu, better known as Sunzi[1] (Sun Tzu in the old style Romanization), a general and strategist in the service of King He Lü of Wu during the Spring and Autumn Annals period of ancient China (770–476 BCE). The accuracy of this version is, however, a matter of heated scholarly debate, with some experts believing that inconsistencies and anachronisms in the text point to a later date of composition, and others questioning even the existence of Sunzi as a historical figure. Further confusing the matter is the existence of a later text from the second half of the fourth century BCE, also called the *Art of War*, written by a man called Sun Bin, who was also known as Sunzi.

---

[1] Throughout the text wherever Chinese names or other words appear, I have adopted the modern pinyin romanization. Thus Sunzi rather than the traditional form Sun Tzu. Although doubts may be raised about the historical authenticity of the attribution, the author of *The Art of War* is traditionally believed to be Sun Wu, known later as Sunzi, a distinguished general in the service of King He Lü of Wu in the sixth century BCE during the Spring and Autumn Annals period (770 – 476 BCE). The content of the text and the types of warfare it describes, however, suggest to many scholars that it was in fact written in the later Warring States period (475 – 221 BCE).

CONTENTS

> **66** [*The Art of War*] ... is divided into 13 chapters, each addressing an aspect of organization or strategic planning. **99**

There is no definitive standard text of *The Art of War*; over centuries of copying, minor variations have crept in, as is the case with most ancient manuscripts. Furthermore, classical Chinese was written without punctuation, which serves to increase the number of possible readings. There are also a number of places where the text is indisputably corrupt. All this, added to the potential ambiguity of the actual language of classical Chinese, means that no two interpretations of *The Art of War* are alike. In this translation I have used one of the most widely accepted versions of the text from the Song Dynasty period (960–1279 CE), and where conflicting interpretations exist, have attempted to allow context and the balance of the prose to dictate my translation.

The structure of the text is generally undisputed. It is divided into 13 chapters, each addressing an aspect of organization or strategic planning. Some of these chapters are more sophisticated and clearly complete than others, indicating again the likelihood of corruption in the text. All of them, however, are at one level intensely practical, especially Sunzi's observations on interpreting the mood of soldiers (both one's own and the enemy's) from their behaviour. What is notable throughout and what raises the work far above a simple military manual is the elegance of the prose and the underlying Daoist principles. In the eyes of Sunzi, a general is no mere jobbing soldier: he is a scholar, gentleman and philosopher. The depth of meaning which this element of mysticism imparts is undoubtedly responsible for the work's continuing and universal appeal.

James Trapp (Translator)

Sunzi Said...

計篇

孫子曰：兵者，國之大事，死生之地，存亡之道，不可不察也。

故經之以五，校之以計，而索其情：一曰道，二曰天，三曰地，四曰 將，五曰法。

計篇

PLANNING

66 War has five decisive factors, which you must take into account in your planning... **99**

Understanding the nature of war is of vital importance to the State. War is the place where life and death meet; it is the road to destruction or survival. It demands study. War has five decisive factors, which you must take into account in your planning; you must fully understand their relevance. First is a Moral Compass; second is Heaven; third is Earth; fourth is the Commander; fifth is Regulation.

道者,令民于上同意者也,可與之死,可與之生,民不 詭也。天者,陰陽、寒暑、時制也。地者,高下、遠近、險易、廣狹、死生也。將者,智、信、仁、勇、嚴也。法者,曲制、官道、主用也。

凡此五者,將莫不聞,知之者勝,不知之者不勝。故校之以計,而索其情。曰:主孰有道?將孰有能?天地孰得?法令孰行?兵眾孰 強?士卒孰練?賞罰孰明?吾以此知勝負矣。

> **❝** ...you must study them when laying your plans and thoroughly understand their relevance. **❞**

A Moral Compass brings the people into accord with their ruler so that they will follow him in life and in death without fear.

Heaven encompasses night and day, heat and cold and the changing of the seasons.

Earth encompasses nearness and distance, ease and hindrance, wide plains and narrow gorges – matters of life or death.

The General must be possessed of wisdom, honesty, benevolence, courage and discipline.[2]

Regulation means the marshalling of the army, correct organization and control of supplies.

A General must pay attention to all five, for they represent the difference between defeat and victory.

So you must study them when laying your plans and thoroughly understand their relevance. By this I mean you should consider:
Which Ruler has a Moral Compass? Which General has ability? Which side is best favoured by climate and terrain? Where is leadership most effective? Which army is strongest? Whose officers and men are best trained? Who best understands the use of reward and punishment? The answers to these questions tell me who will succeed and who will be defeated.

---

[2] Although the *Art of War* is essentially a practical handbook, Sunzi incorporates philosophical principles from both Confucianism and Daoism. The character I have translated as "moral compass" is 道 dào which is the "True Way" of Laozi and Daoism, and clearly here shares something of the same meaning. The five qualities essential in a general are pretty much the military equivalents of the Five Confucian Virtues.

將聽吾計,用之必勝,留之;將不聽吾計,用之必敗,去之。

計利以聽,乃為之勢,以佐其外。勢者,因利而制權也。

兵者,詭道也。故能而示之不能,用而示之不用,近而示之遠,遠而 示之近。利而誘之,亂而取之,實而備之,強而避之,怒而撓之,卑而驕之,佚而勞之,親而離之,攻其不備,出其不意。此兵家之勝, 不可先傳也。

夫未戰而廟算勝者,得算多也;未戰而廟算不勝者,得算少也。多算 勝,少算不勝,而況無算乎!吾以此觀之,勝負見矣。

計篇

> **Successful war follows the path of Deception.**

You should retain those of your generals who heed this advice, for they will be victorious; you should dismiss those who do not, for they will be defeated.

When planning victory according to my counsel, act according to the situation and make use of external factors. To act according to the situation is to seize the advantage by adapting one's plans.

Successful war follows the path of Deception.[3] Thus when you are able to act, feign incapacity; when deploying, feign inactivity; when you are close, appear to be far off; when you are distant, appear close. When your enemy seeks an advantage, lure him further; if he is in disorder, crush him; if he is organized, be ready for him; when he is strong, avoid him; when he is angry, goad him further; if he is humble, be overbearing; if he is resting, harry him; if his armies are united, split them. Attack where he is unprepared, appear where you are least expected. Thus you may see that in war, surprise is the key to victory.

A victorious leader plans for many eventualities before the battle; a defeated leader plans for only a few. Many options bring victory, few options bring defeat, no options at all spell disaster.

It is by using all these considerations that I can foresee who will be victorious and who will be defeated.

---

[3] Sunzi's approach to war is entirely pragmatic; the only aim is to defeat the enemy and there is no concept of anything approaching "chivalry" in describing the means of doing so. The General's "Moral Compass" applies only to his attitude to his ruler.

Sicily, 1943

Sun Tzu reports that a "victorious leader plans for many eventualities before the battle". The Allied forces in World War II enjoyed remarkable success after their amphibious landing at Sicily in 1943, but their victory became a hollow one. Because of a lack of a plan for what to do next, Sicily became an end unto itself.

At the Casablanca Conference in January 1943, the Americans and British committed to an amphibious invasion of Sicily. Other options were considered, but Sicily had several advantages. Its capture would make the Mediterranean safe for shipping, engage and destroy a greater number of German divisions, capture more and better airfields within bombing range of southern Italy, and perhaps cause the Italian government to seek peace.

LIMITED OBJECTIVES

A Sicily operation would satisfy the United States because it would save shipping, employ troops already in theatre, and conclude the Mediterranean campaign. In fact, the Americans accepted Sicily largely because it seemed a dead end. These considerations would facilitate the true US objective: a cross-channel invasion of France. The British agreed to Sicily for shipping considerations, a desire to punish Italy and hope of eliminating Italy from the war. The British were sure that the loss of Sicily would weaken the enemy.

Despite these immediate advantages, Operation Husky was not planned within the context of leading to an overarching strategic objective. At Casablanca, the Allies chose Sicily not because of anything inherent to Sicily but because, as Samuel Morrison concludes, "Something had to be done in the European theater in 1943," and "it was entered upon as an end unto itself; not as a springboard for Italy or anywhere else." The choice "was a strategic compromise conceived in dissension and born of uneasy alliance – a child of conflicting concepts and unclear in purpose." This failure to consider Sicily as part of something bigger than itself ultimately left the Allies with a rather hollow victory.

There was no operational sequel planned as a follow-on to success at Sicily. Part of the reason for this omission was that it had been a difficult process just to agree on Sicily. The participants in the Casablanca Conference did not want to tackle what to do next. As Liddell Hart puts it, "An attempt to decide on the next objective would have revived divergencies of view – but in such matters tactful deferment is apt to result in strategic unreadiness."

The Allies would pay a price for failing to come to terms on a common strategy

Commonwealth troops run through the ruins of Catania, where Montgomery's drive had bogged down. Alexander then authorized Patton to approach Messina from the west, but he too made slow progress against stiffer defences than he had encountered at Palermo.

at the outset. General Omar Bradley, who commanded II Corps during the invasion, wrote: "There were no decisions reached about how to exploit a victory in Sicily... It was an egregious error to leave the future unresolved. It led to misguided planning for and a cloudy conclusion to the Sicily operation and to costly mistakes beyond Sicily."

The Combined Chiefs of Staff were successful in selecting operational commanders at Casablanca. General Dwight Eisenhower would be supreme commander. Admiral Sir Andrew

> ❝ **To act according to the situation is to seize the advantage by adapting one's plans.** ❞

Cunningham would be in command of naval forces, and Air Chief Marshal Sir Arthur Tedder would command air forces. General Sir Harold Alexander would command 15th Army Group, consisting of Seventh Army under General George Patton and Eighth Army under General Sir Bernard Montgomery.

FAILURES IN PLANNING

Eisenhower had his staff immediately begin planning, but not with great effect. One major obstacle was that the commanders were currently engaged in fighting in Tunisia and could not participate in the process. Montgomery described this time as one of "absentee landlordism". General Mark Clark, Fifth Army commander, was more pointed. His diary for 28 April contains the following entry: "It is inexcusable that high planning on an overall scale is not taking definite form. Planners should project themselves forward and set up a grand-scale strategic plan for the Allied forces. We can't win a war by capturing islands."

No significant progress was made at the Trident Conference in May 1943 other than instructing Eisenhower "to plan such operations in exploitation of Husky as are best calculated to eliminate Italy from the war and to contain the maximum number of German forces." Various possible plans beyond Sicily had been discussed, but no decisions were made. Such matters were reserved for the future, in an unfortunate habit of pushing decisions down the road. Trident turned out to be just another stage in a protracted debate rather than a determination.

Despite this ambiguity, an armada of 2590 vessels rendezvoused in the central Mediterranean on 9 July. At 2.45 a.m. on 10 July, the ships reached their debarkation points and began landing troops with almost no resistance from Italian coastal forces. At 6.00 a.m. on 11 July, General Alfredo Guzzoni, who commanded Sixth Italian Army, mounted a counterattack with the Livorno and Herman Goering Divisions. By noon, German tanks were within 2000m (6560ft) of the beach and firing at unloading parties. However, determined resistance and massive naval gunfire forced the Axis units to retreat after losing one-third of their tanks. The following day, Guzzoni began to systematically withdraw to the San Stefano line. His intention was to evacuate Sicily after delaying the Allied forces as much as possible. Still reeling from losses in Stalingrad and Tunisia,

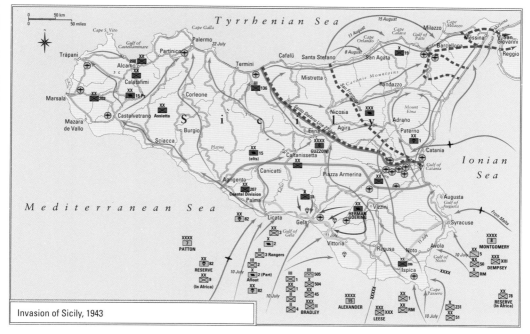

Invasion of Sicily, 1943

Sicily was the second largest amphibious landing of World War II, involving 160,000 men, but the largest in terms of landing area, spread along 170km (105 miles) of coastline.

Hitler opted not to issue his usual hold-at-all-costs order.

Montgomery's attack up the east coast of Sicily was painfully slow and, on 17 July, Patton proposed that his troops overrun western Sicily and take Palermo. Alexander approved and Patton entered the port on 22 July. The following day, he captured the western tip of Sicily. The next day, Alexander ordered Patton to turn eastward towards Messina, the primary transit port between Sicily and the Italian mainland. With Montgomery bogged down at Catania, Alexander redrew the army boundaries, authorizing Patton to approach Messina from the west while Montgomery continued to push from the south. On the morning of 17 August, elements of 7th Infantry Regiment, 3rd Infantry Division, entered Messina.

Sicily was a victory, but, according to Bradley, it had a "cloud on the title". As he claimed, "there was no master plan for the conquest of Sicily. Nothing had been worked out beyond the limited beachhead objectives." Just hours before the Allies reached Messina, the last Axis troops boarded ships for Italy. Sun Tzu advises commanders that "if the enemy leaves you an opening, rush through it". The Allies never had a plan to do so.

作戰篇

孫子曰:凡用兵之法,馳車千駟,革車千乘,帶甲十萬,千里饋糧,則內外之費,賓客之用,膠漆之材,車甲之奉,日費千金,然後十萬 之師舉矣。其用戰也貴勝,久則鈍兵挫銳,攻城則力屈,久暴師則國 用不足。夫鈍兵挫銳,屈力殫貨,則諸侯乘其弊而起,雖有智者,能善其後矣。故兵聞拙速,未睹巧之久也。夫兵久而國利者,未之有也。故不盡知用兵之害者,則不能盡知用兵之利也。

作戰篇

WAGING WAR

❝ Only someone who understands the perils of waging war can also understand the best way of conducting it. ❞

AS FOR MILITARY OPERATIONS, let us consider an army of 1000 attack chariots, 1000 heavy chariots and 100,000 armoured troops, all provisioned for a campaign of 1000 li.[4] Allowing for expenses at headquarters and the front, the entertainment of allies and guests, the cost of glue and lacquer for maintenance and the manufacture of chariots and armour, an army of 100,000 men will require a daily expenditure of 1000 jin.[5]

In waging war, victory is the prize but, if it is delayed, both troops and weapons are blunted; besieging a city exhausts your strength; a protracted campaign depletes the state's resources. With your soldiers and weapons dull, strength and resources spent, your rivals will seize their chance and rise up against you. Then, no matter how wise you are, you can turn nothing to your advantage.

Thus, although I have heard of reckless haste in war, I have never seen wise delay. Nor has any state benefitted from prolonging war. Only someone who understands the perils of waging war can also understand the best way of conducting it.

---

[4] The li is a traditional unit of length in use from the very earliest times; it has, however, varied in value at different periods. Here it equates to approx 400 metres.

[5] The character for jin 金 means "precious metal" and it is not possible to be certain whether it here refers to silver or gold, or indeed what quantity of either.

善用兵者,役不再籍,糧不三載;取用于國,因糧
于敵,故軍食可足 也。

國之貧于師者遠輸,遠輸則百姓貧。近師者貴
賣,貴賣則百姓竭,財 竭則急於丘役。力屈、
財殫,中原内虛于家。百姓之費,十去其七;
公家之費:破軍罷馬,甲胄矢弩,戟盾蔽櫓,丘牛
大車,十去其六。

故智將務食于敵。食敵一鐘,當吾二十鐘;箕杆
一石,當吾二十石。故殺敵者,怒也;取敵之利
者,貨也。故車戰,得車十乘已上,賞其
先得者,而更其旌旗,車雜而乘之,卒善而養之,
是謂勝敵而益強。故兵貴勝,不貴久。

故知兵之將,民之司命,國家安危之主也。

作戰篇

❝ A general who truly understands warfare controls the people's fate. ❞

A skilled general levies troops only once and transports provisions from home only twice. He brings equipment from home but forages for food from the enemy. This is how he keeps his troops fed. Provisioning an army at a distance is a sure way of emptying the state exchequer and beggaring the populace. Prices are inflated by the presence of an army, and inflation swallows up the people's money so that tolls and taxes become oppressive. With strength sapped and wealth depleted, households are stripped bare and the people will lose 70 per cent of their income. As for public finances: broken chariots and broken-down horses, restocking of weapons, shields and armour, draught-oxen and transport wagons, all these will account for 60 per cent of the exchequer.

It is for these reasons that a wise general forages food from the enemy; one zhong of the enemy's food is worth 20 zhong of your own; one dan[6] of the enemy's supplies is worth 20 dan of your own. For your soldiers, anger must be the spur to killing the enemy and reward must be the stimulus to defeating them. Thus in a chariot battle, if ten chariots or more are taken, then reward the soldiers who captured the first one. Change the flags and standards on the captured chariots and add them to your own squadrons. Treat the captured soldiers well and look after them. This is the tactic of using the defeated enemy to increase your strength.

So you can now see that in war it is winning alone that matters and there is no merit in prolonging a campaign. A general who truly understands warfare controls the people's fate. He is the master of the State's security.

---

[6] The zhong was a unit of volume approximately equivalent to 40 litres (8.8 gallons), and the dan a unit of weight approximately equivalent to 50 kilograms (110.2lb).

Zama, 202 BCE

After the Romans suffered disastrous defeats at the hands of Hannibal's Carthaginians at the Battles of Lake Trasimene and Cannae, the Second Punic War dragged on without either side able to achieve final victory. According to Sun Tzu, prolonging a campaign is bad policy, and both the Romans and the Carthaginians would have preferred not to extend the war. Yet Hannibal could not take Rome itself, and the Romans could not drive the Carthaginians out of Italy. The deliberate delaying doctrine of Fabius served Rome well enough for thirteen years, harassing Hannibal without confronting him in major battle.

The Consul Scipio, his prestige much enhanced by his victories against the Carthaginians in Spain, argued for a direct invasion of Africa (present-day Tunisia), with the capital of Carthage as the target. Only in this way could the war be finally ended with a victory for Rome. As Sun Tzu would have said, it is winning alone that matters.

Many in the Roman Senate argued that such a bold course was too dangerous, although some senators supported the idea. Lending weight to Scipio's proposal was the fact that such an invasion was feasible due to Roman control of the sea – an advantage Rome had gained by the end of the First Punic War. Scipio also gained the support of 7000 veteran volunteers, who joined the forces he was gathering in Sicily. The Senate decided to authorize the invasion, with Sicily serving as Scipio's base. The Roman army there included the remnants of the 5th and 6th Legions, survivors of Cannae; they were seasoned veterans with a score to settle with Hannibal.

Vital to Roman prospects in Africa was the new alliance with Numidian Chief Massinissa, as the Numidians had formerly been allied with Carthage. The Numidians were excellent light cavalry, and Massinissa joined forces with Scipio when the Romans arrived in Africa in 203 BCE. This represented an augmentation of about 4000 first-rate horsemen.

Scipio's army moved quickly from the coast and won the Battle of the Great Plains. Sun Tzu would have approved of Scipio's methods at this point. "A skilled general levies troops only once and transports provisions from home only twice. He brings equipment from home but forages for food from the enemy." This is almost precisely what Scipio did.

HANNIBAL GATHERS HIS FORCES
With the threat to Carthage itself imminent, Hannibal was urgently recalled from Italy with as many troops as he could bring. Meanwhile, the Carthaginians hastily raised an army of new recruits,

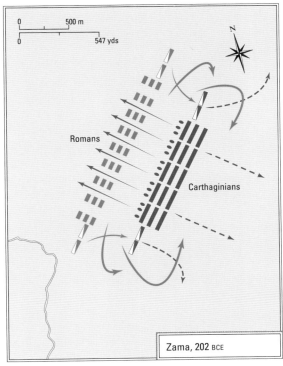

Zama, 202 BCE

At the Battle of Zama, the Roman cavalry (in red) on the flanks routed their opponents, while the Carthaginian elephants were herded between the Roman legion formations and rendered ineffective. In the infantry battle that followed, the superior training and discipline of the Roman legions overcame the Carthaginian mercenaries.

as well as mercenaries. To lend this army some weight, both literally and figuratively, a force of 80 war elephants was organized. Some of these war elephants may not have been as fully trained as per the usual Carthaginian standards. Hannibal took charge of this army in time to command it and bar the path to the city of Carthage.

The opposing armies met at Zama in 202 BCE (probably in October): the outcome of the whole war was very much at stake. Some Roman sources put the strength of Hannibal's army at over 50,000, but it was probably no more than 40,000 men at most. This gave Hannibal a slight numerical edge over Scipio, who had roughly 35,000 troops. One advantage that Scipio had was in cavalry: he had some 6100 good horsemen, including Romans and Numidians, compared to Hannibal's almost 4000 cavalry, which included some Numidians loyal to him.

Each side organized its infantry in three main lines, with cavalry on the flanks. Hannibal placed his mercenary infantry in the first line, his new Carthaginian recruits in the second line, and his veteran troops in the third line, as a reserve. Three main lines of Roman infantry was standard practice at the time, with *hastati* in front, *principe* in the second rank, and heavy *triarii* as a reserve. Light infantry *velites* formed a screen in front of these three main lines.

Hannibal placed his 80 elephants in front of his main lines, with orders to attack and disorder the Roman formations. Some of the elephants, unfortunately for Hannibal, were panicked by Roman trumpets and ran

23

66 So you can now see that in war it is winning alone that matters and there is no merit in prolonging a campaign. 99

in the wrong direction, right into the Carthaginian cavalry on Hannibal's left. Massinissa, with his own Numidian cavalry opposing Hannibal's left, took this opportunity to charge and repulse the Carthaginian cavalry, pursuing them from the field. The rest of the elephants charged the Roman lines, but Scipio had anticipated their attack. The Roman *velites* purposefully screened gaps between Scipio's maniple formations, and then fell back into the gaps, leading the elephants to charge in between Roman formations. The elephants and riders then found themselves showered with javelins and pila from all sides, as the Romans sealed off the gaps behind the elephants before any other Carthaginian forces could come to their aid. A key component of Carthaginian force had been neutralized and eliminated.

Meanwhile, the Roman cavalry on Scipio's left under Laelius also successfully attacked Hannibal's cavalry opposing them and pursued them from the field, as Massinissa had done on the other flank. This left the Carthaginian and Roman infantry to fight out the battle in the centre of the field. This was a fierce fight: the Romans, although somewhat outnumbered, had an advantage of a

higher percentage of veteran troops, while the Carthaginians relied heavily on their mercenaries and new recruits.

Both generals skilfully kept their reserves in hand until the first two Carthaginian lines had been driven back. A lull in the battle followed, as Hannibal rallied his first two lines, placing them on his flanks, with his veteran reserves moved into the centre of his reformed lines. This would have dangerously overlapped Scipio's lines, but Scipio moved his reserves to his own flanks, effectively countering Hannibal.

A DECISIVE VICTORY

With battle between opposing infantry forces rejoined, Massinissa with his Numidians, along with the Roman cavalry under Laelius, suddenly returned to the main field directly behind Hannibal's lines. The Carthaginian cavalry had been pursued well off the field, but Massinissa and Laelius wisely decided that the presence of their own cavalry on the main field of battle was essential. Their timing was decisive, as Hannibal's hard-pressed infantry cracked under the pressure of being attacked front and rear.

The battle quickly turned into a crushing Roman victory, as the

This 16th century tapestry shows Carthaginian elephants fighting with Roman cavalry at the Battle of Zama. In reality, the elephants were neutralised by superior Roman tactics.

Carthaginians were routed. The path to Carthage lay open. The war was won. In the words of Sun Tzu, it is winning alone that matters. To those ends, the Romans under Scipio had pursued and gained a decisive victory with a bold invasion, designed to end a war that had been prolonged too long.

謀攻篇

孫子曰：凡用兵之法，全國為上，破國次之；全軍為上，破軍次之；全旅為上，破旅次之；全卒為上，破卒次之；全伍為上，破伍次之。是故百戰百勝，非善之善也；不戰而屈人之兵，善之善者也。

謀攻篇

STRATEGIC OFFENCE

IN CONSIDERING THE COMPLETE ART OF WAR, it is greatly preferable to capture a state whole rather than break it up; it is better to capture an army whole rather than break it up; it is better to capture a regiment whole rather than break it up; it is better to capture a battalion whole rather than break it up; it is better to capture a company whole rather than break it up. Using this principle, you can understand that winning a hundred victories out of a hundred battles is not the ultimate achievement; the ultimate achievement is to defeat the enemy without even coming to battle.

66 ...it is better to capture an army whole rather than break it up... 99

故上兵伐謀，其次伐交，其次伐兵，其下攻城。攻城之法為不得已。修櫓轒輼〕、具器械、三月而後成，距闉，又三月而後已。將不勝其忿，而蟻附之，殺士三分之一，而城不拔者，此攻之災也。故善用兵者，屈人之兵而非戰也。拔人之城而非攻也，破人之國而非久也，必以 全爭于天下，故兵不頓，而利可全，此謀攻之法也。

故用兵之法，十則圍之，五則攻之，倍則分之，敵則能戰之，少則能逃之，不若則能避之。故小敵之堅，大敵之擒也。

夫將者，國之輔也。輔周則國必強，輔隙則國必

謀攻篇

❝ ...a skilful general must defeat the enemy without coming to battle... ❞

Thus it follows that the highest form of warfare is to out-think the enemy; next is to break his alliances; then to defeat his armies in battle; the lowest form is to besiege his cities. Siege warfare should only be undertaken if it is unavoidable. The time involved is too costly: it takes up to three months to construct the various moveable shelters, transports and other siege engines; it takes another three months to raise earthworks against the walls. If the general loses patience and sends his men swarming like ants around the city, it will cost him a third of his army with no result. These are the disastrous pitfalls of a siege.

Thus a skilful general must defeat the enemy without coming to battle, take his cities without a siege and overthrow his state without a long campaign. He must make every effort under Heaven to achieve total victory with his forces undiminished: this is the art of strategic offence.

Thus, when deploying your troops, if you outnumber the enemy ten to one, surround him; five to one, attack him; two to one, split him.[7] If forces are equal, engage him in open battle; if you in turn are slightly outnumbered, evade his advances; if you are heavily outnumbered, withdraw completely. A smaller force, no matter how determined, will always succumb to a larger one.

---

[7] The terse and elliptical nature of classical Chinese means that there are many passages in the text that are open to different interpretations. Sometimes, as here, the possible interpretations are almost opposites. The phrase that I have translated as "split them [the enemy]" is taken by some translators to mean "divide your own force in two", presumably so that you may attack from both front and rear or front and flank. Classical Chinese is, however, a language of balanced constructions, and, when in doubt, I have allowed the text itself to dictate my interpretation, as it does here.

弱。故君之所以患于軍者三：不知軍之不可以進而謂之進，不知軍之不可 以退而謂之退，是為縻軍；不知三軍之事，而同三軍之政者，則軍士 惑矣；不知三軍之權，而同三軍之任，則軍士疑矣。三軍既惑且疑，則諸侯之難至矣，是謂亂軍引勝。

故知勝有五：知可以戰與不可以戰者勝，識眾寡之用者勝，上下同欲 者勝，以虞待不虞者勝，將能而君不御者勝。此五者，知勝之道也。

故曰：知己知彼，百戰不貽；不知彼而知己，一勝一負；不知彼不知 己，每戰必貽。

謀攻篇

> **66** ...knowing when to fight and when not to, brings victory... **99**

The army's commander is the mainstay of the State; if his support is solid, the State will be strong; if his support is flawed, the State will be weak. Indeed, there are three ways a ruler can bring disaster on his army. He may hobble the army by ordering advance or retreat at the wrong time; he may confuse his troops by interfering in military organization without understanding it; he may dishearten his troops by meddling with rank and responsibility without regard to the consequences. If they see the army confused and discomfited, the lesser lords and princes will take advantage and begin to cause trouble. This is called spurning victory by disrupting the army.

There are five keys to victory: knowing when to fight and when not to, brings victory; knowing what to do both when superior in numbers and when outnumbered, brings victory; holding officers and men united in purpose, brings victory; careful preparation to catch the enemy unprepared, brings victory; a skilful general given free rein by the ruler, brings victory. These five together are the true path to success.

Thus we may say that if you know yourself and know your enemy, you will gain victory a hundred times out of a hundred. If you know yourself but do not know your enemy you will meet one defeat for every victory. If you know neither yourself nor your enemy, you will never be victorious.

Granicus, 334 BCE

Alexander the Great's victory at the River Granicus in 334 BCE
brilliantly represents the Macedonian king's combination of brazenness and
strategic acumen in battle. The battle also exemplifies Sun Tzu's variables for
predicting the outcome of war. Alexander was wholly "unrestrained"
in his approach to every battle, siege and seemingly unwinnable scenario he
faced. He was a tactical genius with an army dedicated to the service of his will.
In every significant engagement he faced, Alexander's successes fall into line
with Sun Tzu's points 2–5 above. Even on the question of whether he
always chose wisely when to fight and when to postpone, his
track record proves that fortune favoured boldness.

On a May afternoon in 334, Persian forces, led by the Greek mercenary general Memnon of Rhodes, took up positions on the plain of Adrastea, west of the city of Zeleia, where, at a recent war council (and against Memnon's advice), Persian leadership had decided to face Alexander's invading army head-on. The Persian plan was to foil Alexander in the Troad, at the gates of Asia, before he could threaten the Persian interior.

The Persians encamped above the plain in an area intersected by the deepest and swiftest section of the River Granicus, which would have been in full swell in late spring. The Persians sought to take advantage of their position, holding the high ground on the far side of the river. They were numerically superior to the Macedonians in cavalry; some 20,000 strong. If Alexander dared to cross the river at its deepest point, the Persians were convinced of their ability to ride down and crush his troops as they emerged from the river.

Alexander's forces approached the river. The king surveyed the circumstances. Both he and his lieutenant, Parmenion, knew that the water's depth and the steepness of the river banks would present significant obstacles, especially to the Macedonian infantry; they would have to cross in a loose order that would allow the Persian cavalry to fall upon them as they struggled out of the water. Nevertheless, he ordered his troops into battle array. Parmenion took command of the left wing; Alexander moved to the right.

If the Persians intended to kill Alexander in this, their first battle with him, ending the Macedonian invasion of Asia Minor before it began in earnest, they would have had no problem locating him: the historian Arrian tells us Alexander cut "an unmistakable figure in magnificent armour, attended by his suite with an almost ecstatic reverence."

Alexander prepared to cross the Granicus in late afternoon, with the sun

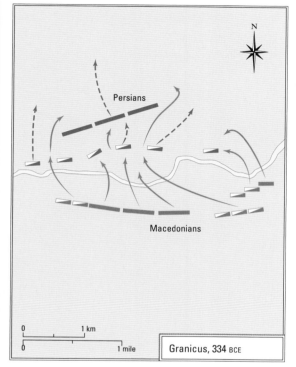

Persians

Macedonians

0   1 km

0   1 mile

Granicus, 334 BCE

At Granicus Alexander employed his usual strategy of attacking the enemy's left of centre with his phalanx of pikemen (in red) while his cavalry harassed from an oblique angle.

in his eyes, at the head of the Companion cavalry, against some 20,000 Persian horses who commanded the high ground on the opposite bank. It was a daring tactic for which Sun Tzu might have praised Alexander, for it played directly into his military strength.

THE FIRST SKIRMISH

First, Alexander ordered his light-armed skirmishing force (*prodromoi*) to cross the river. They needed to get across as quickly as possible to minimize their losses and so likely crossed the river via a ford of some sort. These *prodromoi* were experienced at advance scouting and close-quartered, hand-to-hand fighting. As such, they were directed to distract and/

or engage the Persian cavalry. As the *prodromoi* emerged from the water, they were met with continuous volleys of missiles from the Persians from the high ground of the river bank. Despite some losses, the Macedonians gained the river bank and hand-to-hand struggle ensued.

At this point, Alexander, at the head of the right wing, advanced into the river himself. Parmenion's forces on the left and the Macedonian heavy infantry followed. With the Persian cavalry brought down from their commanding position and onto the plain, their tactical advantage was eliminated. As Alexander and the main Macedonian force strode out of the Granicus, the Persians were forced to make a swift and decisive strategic manoeuvre. They spread out their cavalry ranks so as to cover as wide a swath of ground possible, sending the thickest ranks right at Alexander.

Memnon and his sons appear to have led the main faction of cavalry squadrons. Their aim was surely to take Alexander out quickly, thereby demoralizing and

" ...careful preparation to catch the enemy unprepared, brings victory... "

confusing the Macedonians, for whom the slightest misstep would have meant being pushed back into the Granicus. The Persians nearly regained the upper hand, as Alexander and his immediate retinue were thrust into an enemy onslaught. Alexander's cavalry *sarissa* (the Macedonian long spear) was broken in half, even before a daring charge against the Macedonians' far left by Mithridates, the son-in-law of Darius, the Great King of Persia – a canny outflanking manoeuvre that attempted to press Alexander's forces while they were already engaged with Memnon's.

Alexander's attire was probably intended to make him as prominent as possible, so that the Persians would come at the king first, thereby giving Parmenion and the main thrust of the Macedonian infantry forces time to cross the river unmolested. In fact, Parmenion's troops were hardly needed. When Alexander caught sight of the charging Mithridates, he asked for a new spear. With this new weapon, Alexander disengaged, rallied his men, and rode straight for Mithradates and his oncoming cavalry charge.

ATTACKING ALEXANDER

Alexander struck Mithridates in the face with his spear, knocking him from his horse. Then another Persian commander, Rhoesaces, fell upon Alexander, his scimitar upraised, and struck at Alexander's head. This sliced off a portion of Alexander's protective headgear, leaving him dazed and vulnerable. Alexander recovered enough to fell Rhoesaces with a spear thrust to the chest, but the head blow stunned the Macedonian king, and he does not seem to have registered the Persian warhorse tramping up behind him.

Spithridates, the satrap of Lydia and Ionia, approaching from Alexander's rear, raised his scimitar to deal Alexander what likely would have been his death blow, had not Cleitus "the Black", a commander in the royal squadron of the Companions, rode in and sliced off Spithridates' arm at the shoulder. At this point, a woozy Alexander may have fallen from his horse, to be surrounded swiftly and revived by members of the Companions. He was soon well enough to join the fighting again and lead a rout of the Persian cavalry before the Macedonian heavy infantry had a chance to join battle in earnest.

With the Persian cavalry in retreat, the weaker infantry forces at the Persian centre began to crumble. Memnon ordered the men under his command, mostly Greek mercenaries, to retreat to

This 17th century painting by Charles Le Brun shows Alexander in the thick of the battle at Granicus River. He was famous for leading from the front, often drawing the heaviest attacks of the enemy upon himself.

the high ground above the plain and wait. They watched as their Persian employers fled before Alexander.

Memnon sent a message to Alexander asking for terms of surrender, which Alexander refused to provide. Instead, he called upon his phalanx – still fresh from lack of serious fighting – to attack Memnon's position. Despite his heavy involvement in the earlier fighting, Alexander led the frontal assault himself. Memnon's mercenaries fought valiantly: it was clear that Alexander would show them no mercy. Alexander was harsh towards the disloyal and surely felt that Greek mercenaries had no business fighting for the Great King of Persia.

Although the Macedonians ultimately defeated his men, Memnon managed to escape and trouble Alexander another day. But this day was Alexander's. He had struck the first blow that would lead to the collapse of a 250-year-old empire. He had done so through a keen understanding of circumstances and geography; by a bold gambit that made himself bait; and by predicting the response of his opposition.

The Battle of the Granicus illustrates perfectly Sun Tzu's notion of strategic offence. It also demonstrated that the Macedonians and their king were a singularly focused, highly co-ordinated martial collective whose equal the world had not yet seen.

形篇

孫子曰：昔之善戰者，先為不可勝，以侍敵之可勝。不可勝在己，可 勝在敵。故善戰者，能為不可勝，不能使敵之必可勝。故曰：勝可知，而不可為。不可勝者，守也；可勝者，攻也。守則不足，攻則有餘。善守者，藏于九地之下；善攻者，動于九天之上。故能自保而全勝 也。

形篇

DEPLOYMENT

" Whilst you are unsure of victory, defend; when you are sure of victory, attack. "

THE GREAT GENERALS OF OLD first ensured that they themselves were beyond defeat and then waited for the enemy to make themselves vulnerable. Thus we can say that although you have it in your own hands to place yourself beyond defeat, you cannot, of yourself, bring about the defeat of the enemy. Whilst you are unsure of victory, defend; when you are sure of victory, attack. Defence should indicate that you are not in a position to defeat the enemy, attack that you are even stronger than you need to be. A skilled defender digs himself in deeper than the ninth level of the Earth; a skilled attacker falls on the enemy from above the ninth level of Heaven.[8] In this way you can both protect yourself completely and ensure total victory.

---

[8] The ultimate level of heaven in Buddhist mythology.

見勝不過眾人之所知, 非善之善者也; 戰勝而天下曰善, 非善之善者也。故舉秋毫不為多力, 見日月不為明目, 聞雷霆不為聰耳。古之所謂善戰者, 勝于易勝者也。故善戰之勝也, 無智名, 無勇功。故其戰 勝不忒。不忒者, 其所措必勝, 勝已敗者也。故善戰者, 立于不敗之地, 而不失敵之敗也。是故勝兵先勝而後求戰, 敗兵先戰而後求勝。善用兵者, 修道而保法, 故能為勝敗之政。

兵法: 一曰度, 二曰量, 三曰數, 四曰稱, 五曰勝。地生度, 度生量, 量生數, 數生稱, 稱生勝。故勝兵若以鎰稱銖, 敗兵若以銖稱鎰。
勝者之戰民也, 若決積水于千仞之谿者, 形也。

形篇

> **A successful army first ensures invincibility, and only then engages the enemy.**

Only to see victory when it is already clear to all is by no means the height of excellence; a victory that is acclaimed by all and sundry is by no means the greatest of victories. It takes no great strength to lift a feather; you don't need keen eyesight to see the sun, nor keen ears to hear thunder. The great warriors of old not only won victories, but won them with ease; because their victories were achieved without apparent difficulty, they did not bring them great fame for their wisdom or respect for their courage. Being prepared for all circumstances is what ensures certain victory, for it means you are fighting an enemy who is already beaten. Thus a great soldier first places himself in an invincible position, and then ensures he does not miss the crucial opportunity to defeat the enemy. A successful army first ensures invincibility, and only then engages the enemy. A vanquished army will have gone into battle first, and only then looked for the means of victory. A great strategist follows his Moral Compass and adheres to his methods of Regulation, for these are the means by which he determines victory or defeat.

In the Art of War, first comes scoping, then measurement, then calculation, then balancing[9] and finally victory. The Earth is the basis for scoping, scoping the basis for measurement, measurement the basis for calculation, calculation the basis for balancing, and balancing the basis for victory. A victorious army is just as an yi is to a shu, and a defeated army is as a shu to an yi.[10] A victorious army carries all the weight of flood water plunging into a thousand-foot gorge.

---

[9] The translation of these four terms is, again, my own interpretation as any precise technical meaning for the original Chinese characters has been lost. What is clearly implied is a process from general to specific, or from broad-brush to fine detail.

[10] An yi is a unit of weight approximating to 500 grams (1.1lb) and a shu is approximately 1 gram (0.035oz).

Gulf War, 1990–91

**The First Gulf War (1990–91) provides a useful case study to illustrate
Sun Tzu's ruminations on the role of deployment in military strategy.
The term "deployment" refers to the allocation and positioning of forces
within the battle space and the relationship of these realities to the strategic
planning and conduct of a military campaign. Sun Tzu's thoughts
on deployment revolved around the idea that "a successful army first
ensures invincibility, and only then engages the enemy." If one of the
belligerents in a conflict followed such a strategy, this
would enable them to win victory with ease.**

On 2 August 1990, President Saddam Hussein's Iraqi Army invaded and occupied its tiny southern neighbour, Kuwait. Saddam wished to acquire the country's wealth to offset the huge debts incurred during the Iran–Iraq War (1980–88). With the Cold War ending, consensus emerged within the United Nations, which demanded an immediate Iraqi withdrawal. Subsequent UN Resolutions authorized economic sanctions against Iraq and the defensive deployment of an American-led multinational military coalition to prevent further Iraqi aggression. This deployment, commanded by American General Norman Schwarzkopf, became Operation Desert Shield and eventually reached a strength of 550,000 troops.

OPERATION DESERT SHIELD

As sanctions had not forced an Iraqi withdrawal by late October 1990, America decided to use military force. Early Coalition offensive action was just about practicable. However, when the Americans war-gamed the then-strategic campaign plan (the single-corps plan), which was finalized in early November, they were reasonably confident of securing success within three weeks, but at significant cost in casualties.

On 8 November, instead of initiating this campaign, the Coalition decided to push back their plans and strengthen their forces by redeploying the US VII Corps from Germany. When they war-gamed the two-corps offensive plan, the result was an anticipated quicker victory, with significantly lower casualties. This Coalition strategy reflected Sun Tzu's advice that "whilst you are unsure of victory, defend".

While VII Corps redeployed to the Gulf during November, the UN increased the political pressure on Saddam, authorizing on 29 November military action to reverse the Iraqi invasion. This Resolution gave the Iraqis the deadline of 15 January 1991 to withdraw. This seven-week window

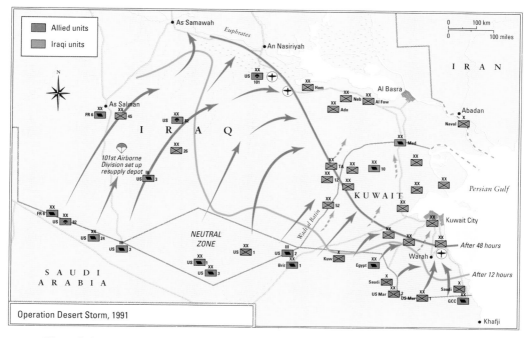

Map of the Coalition advance, 24–26 February 1991. Out in the west US VII Corps' "left hook" envelopment is clear, with its spearheads approaching the main mass of Republic Guard divisions west of Basra.

gave the Coalition time to absorb VII Corps' arrival and refine their two-corps campaign plan. As the Iraqis had not begun withdrawing from Kuwait on the expiry of this deadline, the Coalition air campaign commenced on the night of 16/17 January 1991.

THE AIR CAMPAIGN

By initiating an air (rather than a ground) campaign, the Coalition played to their strengths and thus obeyed Sun Tzu's dictum that attackers should "protect themselves completely". The Coalition air war, which lasted for 39 days

without ground action commencing, combined strategic attacks on Baghdad with attritional efforts to weaken the Iraqi ground forces to the 50 per cent strength level that had been set as the prerequisite for starting the ground war. This aerial-delivered softening up of the Iraqi Army before the ground offensive began reflected Sun Tzu's advice that "a great soldier first places himself in an invincible position" before launching his offensive actions. The air campaign, which delivered 85,350 tonnes (84,000 tons) of munitions, effectively attrited the Iraqi ground forces: it inflicted 126,000 troop

41

In February 1991 images such as this appeared, apparently showing the mass destruction inflicted by Coalition aircraft on Iraqi vehicles fleeing from Kuwait north along the Basra Road (the "Highway of Death").

casualties (including 86,000 surrendered/ deserted), destroyed 450 tanks and degraded Iraqi command and resupply capabilities by 90 per cent.

Under the cover of total aerial superiority, the Coalition had covertly conducted a major redeployment. Its main strike force, US VII Corps, was redeployed from the east of the theatre out to the far western flank. This clever redeployment effectively outflanked the static Iraqi defences along the Kuwaiti–Saudi and Iraqi–Saudi borders. Some even thought

that the Iraqis had sensibly followed Sun Tzu's thought that "a skilled defender digs himself in deeper than the ninth level of the Earth". The Coalition's outflanking of these defences ensured they also followed the ancient strategist's guidance that the "skilled attacker falls on the enemy from above the ninth level of Heaven".

THE COALITION STRIKES
On 24 February, US Marine formations, supported by Arab forces, launched a powerful subsidiary attack in the east of

the theatre into the heart of the Iraqi defences that blocked the direct route towards Kuwait City. Simultaneously, other US Marine forces maintained the deception of an impending amphibious assault on the Kuwaiti coast to "fix" the Iraqis' attention in the east; the heavy defensive screens slowed the Coalition advance and inflicted some casualties. Nine hours later, VII Corps initiated its own offensive, bypassing around the western flank of the main Iraqi defensive screen and charging northeasterly as rapidly as possible. These quickly advancing Coalition divisions brought heavy fire down on the enemy units they encountered, with battle tanks, aviation assets and close-support tactical aircraft; this soon broke enemy will to resist. Meanwhile, to prevent the Iraqis

An Iraqi ex-Chinese Type 69 main battle tank burns fiercely. Coalition rotary/fixed-winged platforms and ground-based indirect and direct fires all proved devastatingly effective, helping the Coalition achieve "invincibility".

" The great warriors of old not only won victories, they won them with ease. "

A Coalition interceptor "force package" with F-16A Fighting Falcon, F-15E Strike Eagle and F-15C Eagle fighters flying across Kuwait's open desert terrain; in the background a number of oil wells burn fiercely.

bringing in reinforcements or escaping north across the Euphrates River, the 101st US Air Assault Division established forward-operating bases astride Highway 8 along the Euphrates valley. Continuing to exploit surprise and shock during 25 February, VII Corps' five divisions rapidly overran the Iraqi reserves and began to wheel eastward so as to engage Saddam's Republican Guard divisions, positioned astride the Iraqi–Kuwaiti border's northwestern segment.

On 26 February, in the Battle of the 73rd Easting, VII Corps' spearheads smashed into the Tawakalna Republican Guard division. The Tawakalna resisted fiercely and even launched determined counterattacks; in a battle that see-sawed for hours, the Coalition forces annihilated an entire Iraqi brigade. With VII Corps continuing to advance eastward on 27 February into the main Republican Guard positions, Iraqi resistance elsewhere began to collapse.

By the early hours of 28 February – the fourth day of the war – the Coalition had liberated all of Kuwait bar the northeastern corner. By then, Iraqi resistance had totally collapsed, and their battered remnants fled north in a disorganized retreat. Thus, at 0800 on 28 February 1991, General Schwarzkopf announced a ceasefire, halting the ground war 100 hours after it had commenced. The main intent of the ground campaign plan was that VII Corps would engage and destroy the Republican Guard; however, Schwarzkopf shut down the war just as VII Corps was preparing to initiate this last climactic engagement.

In just 100 hours of fast-paced, technologically advanced, armoured warfare, the Coalition had inflicted a devastating defeat on Saddam's forces, which suffered in excess of 180,000 casualties, including 130,000 prisoners of war. Coalition casualties were astonishingly low – a mere 2000. In part, this success owed much to the Coalition's execution of military principles that accorded with Sun Tzu's discourses on deployment. The Coalition had indeed defended "when they were unsure of victory", and then redeployed VII Corps from Germany so that they could, from "an invincible position" commence their offensive now that they were "sure of victory". Consequently, the scale and speed of the Coalition victory meant that the 1991 Gulf War reflected Sun Tzu's declaration that the apogee of military strategy was achieved by "great warriors [who] not only won great victories, but won them with ease."

勢篇

孫子曰：凡治眾如治寡，分數是也；鬥眾如鬥寡，形名是也；三軍之 眾，可使必受敵而無敗，奇正是也；兵之所加，如以碬投卵者，虛實是也。

勢篇

MOMENTUM

❝ To make the force of your army's attack like a grindstone crushing an egg, you must master the substantial and the insubstantial. ❞

THE PRINCIPLES OF CONTROL for a large force are the same as for a small one; the essential factor is how they are divided up. Deploying a large army in battle is just like deploying a small one; it is a matter of formation and communication. To hold an entire army unbroken in the face of enemy attack is achieved by use of both the oblique and the direct. To make the force of your army's attack like a grindstone crushing an egg, you must master the substantial and the insubstantial.[11]

---

[11] The following two chapters are crucial to understanding Sunzi's approach to war. He uses two pairs of terms "zheng" 正 and "qi" 奇, and "shi" 實 and "xu" 虛 which are very challenging to translate with the full weight of meaning the Chinese carries. Underlying both pairs is the understanding that apparent opposites are, in fact, part of the same continuum, and that in harnessing one aspect you are also automatically involving the other. Thus, in translating "shi" and "xu" as substantial and insubstantial, we should really understand them as that which appears to have substance or weight and that which appears not to. Equally with "zheng" and "qi" superficial appearances mask a different reality where it is the indirect that actually achieves the purpose whilst the direct merely holds a position or distracts attention. Since these terms are part of a continuum, their meanings may also be relative. Something that is insubstantial to the defender may in fact be substantial to the attacker, and something that appears direct to one army is in fact indirect to the one opposing it. To Sunzi, much of the art of skilled leadership lies in harnessing these paradoxes.

凡戰者，以正合，以奇勝。故善出奇者，無窮如天地，不竭如江河。終而復始，日月是也。死而復生，四時是也。聲不過五，五聲之變，不可勝聽也。色不過五，五色之變，不可勝觀也。味不過五，五味之變，不可勝嘗也。戰勢不過奇正，奇正之變，不可勝窮之也。奇正相生，如環之無端，孰能窮之？

激水之疾，至于漂石者，勢也；鷙鳥之疾，至于毀折者，節也。是故善戰者，其勢險，其節短。勢如張弩，節如發機。

In all kinds of warfare, the direct approach is used for attack, but the oblique is what achieves victory. A general who understands the use of the oblique has a source of tactics as inexhaustible as Heaven and Earth, which, like the Rivers and the Oceans, will never run dry. Like the Sun and Moon, they diminish and then replenish; they constantly renew themselves like the cycle of the Four Seasons. There are only five basic notes in music,[12] but their variations are infinite. There are only five primary colours,[13] but when blended, their shades and hues are limitless. There are only five principal tastes,[14] but their combinations produce more flavours than can ever be tasted. In military strategy, there is only the direct and the oblique, but between them they offer an inexhaustible range of tactics. The direct and the oblique lead naturally one into the other, like an ever-turning wheel, so who can ever exhaust their resource? The surge of rolling flood-water washes away boulders: this is called momentum. The swoop of a falcon strikes and kills its prey: this is called timing. Thus for a skilled warrior, his momentum must be irresistible and his timing precise. Momentum is the tension in a crossbow arm; timing is the pulling of the trigger.

> **66 The swoop of a falcon strikes and kills its prey: this is called timing. 99**

---

[12] Ancient Chinese music worked with a pentatonic scale.

[13] Red, blue, yellow, black and white.

[14] Sweet, salty, sour, bitter and savouriness – the last is now known as "umami".

紛紛紜紜,鬥亂而不可亂也。渾渾沌沌,形圓而不可敗也。亂生于治,怯生于勇,弱生于強。治亂,數也;勇怯,勢也;強弱,形也。故善動敵者,形之,敵必從之;予之,敵必取之。以利動之,以卒動 之。

故善戰者,求之于勢,不責于人,故能擇人而任勢。任勢者,其戰人 也,如轉木石。木石之性,安則靜,危則動,方則止,圓則行。故善戰人之勢,如轉圓石于千仞之山者,勢也。

勢篇

" Confusion and organization are a matter of deployment. "

In the rolling turmoil of battle, your troops may appear to be in chaos, but in fact cannot be disordered; in tumult and confusion, your dispositions may seem formless, but in fact remain invincible. In this way, apparent confusion masks true organization; cowardice masks courage; weakness masks strength. Confusion and organization are a matter of deployment. Cowardice and courage are a matter of momentum. Strength and weakness are a matter of formation. A general skilled in out-manoeuvring the enemy uses formation to make them follow him; he offers a sacrifice to make them snatch at it; he lays bait to tempt them and sets his troops in ambush to wait for them.[15]

The skilled general seeks combined momentum and does not rely on individual prowess; he knows how to choose his men for maximum combined effect. This combined effect in battle has the power of rolling logs and boulders. It is the nature of logs and boulders to remain still on level ground, but to roll down a slope; they will come quickly to a halt if they have squared-off sides, but keep rolling if they are round. The momentum of skilled warriors is like a round boulder tumbling down a thousand-foot mountain. This is what I have to say on momentum.

---

[15] This paragraph is one of the most difficult to translate in the whole text. I offer my version as being in keeping both with the structure of the original Chinese and with the overall tenor of Sunzi's approach, but make no claim to it being definitive.

Vistula–Oder Offensive, January 1945

The January 1945 Soviet Vistula–Oder offensive, which annihilated the German defences in Poland, provides an excellent case study of Sun Tzu's thought on "momentum". Contemporary Western military doctrine views momentum as the impact of an advancing force on the enemy; its impact is determined by its mass and the speed of advance. This reflects Sun Tzu's description of momentum as "a round boulder tumbling down a thousand-foot mountain".

The idea of increasing forward offensive momentum was reflected in the Soviets' conduct of the Vistula–Oder offensive. The Soviet spearheads advanced on slightly divergent axes, widening the frontage of the offensive; this created the space regularly to feed reserve units into the contact battle in what was termed "the expanding torrent". Even the name of this practice echoed Sun Tzu's "surging flood-water" metaphor. The offensive, moreover, epitomized Sun Tzu's homily that the attacker's momentum "must be irresistible". The execution of the offensive also reflected the modern doctrinal notion of "the Manoeuvrist Approach" – executing unrelenting offensive action swiftly to break enemy will and cohesion, of which the generation of "momentum" is a key tenet. Through these tactics, the offensive achieved an incredible victory while incurring only modest casualties.

UNRELENTING OFFENSIVE

In early January 1945, the 2.3 million Axis troops deployed on the Eastern Front faced 6 million Soviet soldiers. By then, powerful Soviet forces had assembled in three bridgeheads that had been established across the River Vistula in central Poland: at Baranov (in Marshal Konev's First Ukrainian Front sector) and further north at Magnuszew and Pulawy (in the sector manned by Marshal Zhukov's First White Russian Front).

On 12 January, 1.57 million Soviet troops, 6410 AFVs, and 46,100 guns faced 400,559 German soldiers backed by 1156 AFVs and 4123 artillery guns. The Ninth Army held the 176-km (102-mile) sector from Warsaw down to Pulawy, while the Fourth Panzer Army held the192-km (119-mile) front down to Baranov. Between the front line and the River Oder, moreover, there existed nine recently constructed German rear defensive lines, manned by only a few Home Guard battalions. The Soviet offensive, therefore, aimed to generate high forward momentum, so that its spearheads might penetrate these defences before the Germans could adequately man them.

**ПОД ЗНАМЕНЕМ ЛЕНИНА—
К ПОЛНОЙ ПОБЕДЕ!**

**The Soviets used
extensive propaganda
to encourage both
the Red Army and
civilians to redouble
their efforts to defeat
the Axis invader.
This poster evokes
the spirit of the
father of the 1917
Bolshevik Revolution,
Vladimir Lenin.**

Konev's Front initiated the offensive from Baranov on 12 January with an intense artillery barrage; subsequently, 18 rifle divisions, backed by armour, assaulted the German line and swiftly secured deep penetrations. Behind these forces, Konev husbanded his second assault echelon – 31 armoured brigades. Recognizing the scale of initial Soviet success, Konev brought his plans forward so that the offensive momentum could be maximized. Astonishingly, that night all 31 of Konev's mobile reserve armoured brigades successfully passed through his 18 in-contact rifle divisions. Over the next day, these armoured brigades smashed through the German tactical reserves, destroyed four German divisions, and surged unstoppably westward.

Having drawn the few German operational reserves southward towards Baranov, on 14 January Zhukov's forces

at Magnuszew and Pulawy assaulted the
Ninth Army's positions and secured a
21-km (13-mile) westward advance.
After similarly swiftly committing his
reserve armoured brigades, Zhukov's
spearheads charged westward a further
56km (35 miles) over the ensuing
three days. Having overrun the few
German reserves, little now stood in
the way of Zhukov's spearheads as they
raced westward, maintaining forward
momentum so as to "bounce through"
the as-yet unmanned German rear area
defensive lines.

During 15–18 January, Konev's and
Zhukov's armoured vanguards charged
westward on slightly divergent axes,
resting only a few hours each night,
to maintain maximum momentum.
On 18 January, the WNW advance of
Konev's right flank linked up with the
WSW advance of Zhukov's left flank; this
permitted the Soviet forces to drive west
along a contiguous 246-km (153-mile)
front. By advancing on slightly divergent
axes, gradually increasing the frontage
over which the offensive unfolded, the
Soviets created space for their third
echelon of armoured deep reserves to
join the battle. Through this "expanding
torrent", the Soviets cumulatively applied
unstoppable combat power.

PROTECTING SILESIA

On 19 January, Konev's vanguards
crossed the pre-1939 Reich border and
approached the Silesian industrial district,
Germany's second great economic centre.
If Germany lost this district, the war would
be over in a few months once existing
stocks had run out. The area thus became
another Führer-declared "fortress" to
be held under any circumstances. Just
two days previously, fulfilling this order
would have been impossible. However,
by desperately throwing into the line
divisions redeployed from elsewhere,
as well as numerous ad-hoc alarm units,
the Germans had partially recovered
their cohesion.

Thus, on 21–26 January, the defending
Germans slowed the Soviet advance
towards the industrial district's eastern
fringes, threatening to undermine the
Soviet risk-taking that had enabled such
forward momentum to be generated
previously. To unhinge the determined
German defence, Konev's spearheads
now suddenly swung left and raced south
towards Rybnik, deep in the German
rear. By 27 January, this advance had left
the Germans defending the industrial
zone virtually trapped in a finger-shaped
northward-running salient; the defenders
now had to extricate themselves rapidly

A troop of T-34/76 tanks surge forward across undulating wintry terrain during early 1945 along the offensive's northern flank in East Prussia. The sheer speed and cross-country capabilities of armoured vehicles were critical for the generation of offensive momentum.

from the salient before becoming encircled. The sudden change of direction ensured that the Silesian industrial zone fell largely intact into Soviet hands.

Meanwhile, the rest of Konev's and Zhukov's forces had raced westward, bouncing successive German defence lines that remained largely unmanned. Consequently, by 31 January, Konev's forces had reached the River Oder across a 296-km (185-mile) front from Glogau down to Ratibor. Having advanced relentlessly for 15 days, Konev's forces were exhausted and now faced a Fourth Panzer Army that had been reinforced by several divisions transferred from elsewhere. Even though this rag-tag force managed to retard Konev's momentum, it could not stop his forces securing five critical bridgeheads over the Oder before Stalin halted the offensive on 3 February.

A TEMPORARY REPRIEVE

Meanwhile, on 19–31 January, Zhukov's armies surged west through the northern Warthegau to reach the Oder between

In a town close to the River Oder during the wintry last days of January 1945 Red Army soldiers prepare to fire an M1927 infantry gun; direct fire proved helpful in dislodging pockets of German resistance, thus facilitating forward momentum.

Küstrin and Frankfurt. Subsequently, by 2 February, Soviet assaults had established two dangerous bridgeheads across the river. However, a rapid thaw now occurred that broke up the frozen Oder and turned the ground into a quagmire. Consequently, on 3 February, Stalin decided to halt the offensive: Zhukov's forces were exhausted and lacked supplies, the thaw hindered their mobility,

the German build-up in Pomerania threatened their northern flank, and the Luftwaffe had temporarily regained local air superiority. Berlin had been reprieved, for the moment.

The Soviet January 1945 Vistula–Oder offensive had effectively combined Sun Tzu's "direct" methods – overwhelming frontal assault in the initial break-in battle fought on 12–14 January – with "oblique"

66 The surge of rolling flood-water washes away boulders: this is called momentum. 99

methods. The latter included combined arms and joint co-operation to generate incredible tempo and momentum to smash German will and cohesion. In part, this was achieved through the "expanding torrent" technique, which reflected Sun Tzu's notion of "the surge of rolling flood-water". In just 22 days, the overwhelming Soviet onslaught had inflicted 400,000 casualties on the Germans and captured most of Poland west of the Vistula. The German capital Berlin was now very much in their sights.

The Soviets used the "expanding torrent" to exploit the success achieved by the Vistula–Oder offensive; here T-34/85 tanks cross the River Elbe via a railway bridge into western Dresden in April 1945.

虛實篇

孫子曰:凡先處戰地而待敵者佚,後處戰地而趨戰者勞。

故善戰者,致人而不致于人。

能使敵自至者,利之也;能使敵不得至者,害之也。故敵佚能勞之,飽能飢之,安能動之。

出其所不趨,趨其所不意。行千里而不勞者,行于無人之地也。攻而 必取者,攻其所不守也。守而必固者,守其所不攻也。

虛實篇

THE SUBSTANTIAL AND THE INSUBSTANTIAL

66 *...a great warrior takes control of others and does not let others control him...* **99**

IT IS A GENERAL PRINCIPLE that the army which arrives first at the site of battle and waits for the enemy will be fresh, and the army that arrives second to the field and has to rush into battle will be laboured and exhausted.

Thus a great warrior takes control of others and does not let others control him.[16] By holding out temptation, he can make the enemy approach; by inflicting harm, he can hold them at a distance. Using the same principles, if the enemy are taking their ease, he can rouse them; if they are well-provisioned, he can starve them; if they are encamped, he can move them on. Attack at points which the enemy must scramble to defend, and launch lightning attacks where they are not expected. It is possible to march your army a thousand li as long as it is across unoccupied territory. To be sure of success, only attack at undefended areas. To be sure in defence, mount your defences at those places the enemy cannot attack.

---

[16] Nowhere in the text is it more evident than here that Sunzi pre-supposes no other master of the art of war exists who might be similarly advising the enemy.

故善攻者,敵不知其所守。善守者,敵不知其所 攻。

微乎微乎,至于無形,神乎神乎,至于無聲,故能為敵之司命。

進而不可御者,沖其虛也;退而不可追者,速而不可及也。故我欲戰,敵雖高壘深溝,不得不與我戰者,攻其所必救也;我不欲戰,雖畫地而守之,敵不得與我戰者,乖其所之也。

故形人而我無形,則我專而敵分;我專為一,敵分為十,是以十攻其 一也,則我眾而敵寡;能以眾擊寡者,則吾之所與戰者,約矣。吾所與戰之地不可知,不可知,則敵所備者多,敵所備者多,則吾之所戰 者,寡矣。

> **66** **Weakness in numbers stems from having to mount defences... 99**

Thus when facing a warrior skilled in attack, the enemy does not know where to defend; with a warrior skilled in defence, they do not know where to attack. Be subtle! Be subtle! You can make yourself invisible. Be secretive! Be secretive! You can move without a sound. Thus you hold the enemy's fate in your hands. To advance without the possibility of being checked, you must strike fast at the enemy's weakest points. To retreat without the possibility of being caught, you must march at a speed the enemy cannot match. If you want to bring the enemy to battle, even though he is entrenched behind the deepest of ditches and highest of ramparts, you must attack at a point he cannot afford not to rally to.

If you do not wish to engage with the enemy, even though your defences are no more than a line in the ground, you can prevent them attacking by luring them away with a feint or a decoy. If you can see the enemy's dispositions, but they cannot see yours, then you can keep your forces united whilst they must split up to allow for all possibilities. If you are a single unit but the enemy is divided into ten, then the odds are ten to one in your favour at any given point. If you have a superior force you can use to attack an enemy's inferior one, then inevitably you outnumber them. If you can keep your point of attack secret from the enemy, then they will be forced to mount defences at many different places. With their forces thus stretched, wherever you attack it will be with superior numbers. If they reinforce their van, they weaken their rear; if they reinforce their left flank, they weaken their right and so on. If they try to reinforce every possible position, then every position will be weakened.

Weakness in numbers stems from having to mount defences; strength in numbers stems from forcing the enemy to mount such defences.

故備前則後寡，備後則前寡，故備左則右寡，備右則左寡，無所不備，則無所不寡。寡者備人者也，眾者使人備己者也。

故知戰之地，知戰之日，則可千里而會戰。不知戰之地，不知戰之日，則左不能救右，右不能救左，前不能救後，後不能救前，而況遠者 數十里，近者數里乎？

以吾度之，越人之兵雖多，亦奚益于勝敗哉？！

故曰：勝可為也。敵雖眾，可使無鬥。

故策之而知得失之計，作之而知動靜之理，形之而知死生之地，角之 而知有餘不足之處。

虛實篇

Thus if you know in advance the time and place of engagement, you can march a thousand li and still join battle. If you do not know the time and place of engagement, then you do not know whether to reinforce your van or your rear, your left or your right flank – imagine the difficulties if your furthest divisions are separated by tens of li, and even if the closest ones are only a few li apart.

By my calculations, the army of Yue[17] outnumbers ours, but this advantage will most surely not bring them victory!

I say that victory will be ours. Even if the enemy outnumber you, you can prevent them from joining battle.

Lay plans to discover the enemy's intentions and their likelihood of success; provoke him to understand the dynamics of his movement and inactivity; force him to deploy where you can study his formations so that you can see his strongpoints and weaknesses; take his measure so that you know where his dispositions are under-manned and where they are over-manned.

In deploying your troops, the greatest skill is in keeping the enemy in the dark. Keep your dispositions secret so that the most thorough of searches cannot discover them and they are hidden from the sharpest of intellects.

---

[17] On occasions Sunzi becomes specific rather than generalizing, and instances such as this one are taken as evidence that he was indeed writing for King He Lü of Wu. It is certainly true that the states of Wu and Yue were at war for a long period from the sixth to early fifth century BCE, culminating in fact in the defeat of Wu in 473 BCE.

故形兵之極, 至于無形;無形, 則深間不能窺, 智者不能謀。

因形而錯勝于眾, 眾不能知;人皆知我所以勝之形, 而莫知吾所以制 勝之形。故其戰勝不復, 而應形于無窮。

夫兵形象水, 水之形避高而趨下, 兵之形, 避實而擊虛, 水因地而制 流, 兵應敵而制勝。故兵無常勢, 水無常形, 能因敵變化而取勝者, 謂之神。

故五行無常勝, 四時無常位, 日有短長, 月有死生。

虛實篇

The common people cannot comprehend how I contrive my victories from the dispositions of the enemy themselves; all they see are the tactics by which victory is won, and none of them understand the planning behind them. Never employ the same strategy twice, but use the infinite variety at your disposal.

Military strategy is like water, which flows away from high ground towards low ground; so, in your tactics, avoid the enemy's strengths and attack his weaknesses. Water adapts its course according to the terrain; in the same way you should shape your victory around the enemy's dispositions. There are no constants in warfare, any more than water maintains a constant shape. Thus a general who gains victory by shaping his tactics according to the enemy ranks with the Immortals.

None of the Five Elements[18] remains dominant for long; none of the Four Seasons lasts indefinitely; the Sun rises and sets; the Moon waxes and wanes.

> **66 There are no constants in warfare, any more than water maintains a constant shape. 99**

---

[18] The Five Elements of traditional Chinese medicine and philosophy: wood, water, earth, metal and fire.

Somalia, 1993

Sun Tzu advises his readers to exploit opportunities that come from the openings in the environment caused by the relative weakness of the enemy in a given area. In the case of Somalia, the American weakness was perseverance. To take advantage of this situation, Aideed did not need to defeat the Americans in a force-on-force battle, only to convince them that the effort was not worth continuing. This he did at the Battle of Mogadishu.

The US involvement in Somalia came as a response to the anarchy, drought, civil war and banditry that had reduced Somalia, a country encompassing approximately 637,540 square kilometres (246,155 square miles) on the Horn of Africa, to a virtual wasteland. Some 300,000 Somalis had died between November 1991 and March 1993, and another 1.5 million lives were at immediate risk because of famine. Nearly 4.5 million of Somalia's six million people were threatened by severe malnutrition and related diseases. Another 700,000 had sought refuge in neighbouring countries.

THWARTED BY WARLORDS

To help relieve the mass starvation, the United Nations Security Council in April 1992 approved Resolution 751, which established a humanitarian aid mission known as United Nations Operation in Somalia (UNOSOM I). UNOSOM I's success was severely limited because Somali warlords, most notably Mohamed Farah Aideed of the Habr Gidr subclan and Ali Mahdi Mohamed of the Abgal subclan, refused full co-operation, and the limited mandate was not strong enough to compel compliance. The warlords kept the UNOSOM I troops from leaving Mogadishu Airport, and only 500 of the authorized 3500 troops deployed.

The failure of UNOSOM I quickly became apparent, and the US found itself under increasing pressure to act. Responding to a variety of motivations, the US won United Nations Security Council approval in December 1992 of Resolution 794, which established Unified Task Force (UNITAF), a large, US-led peace enforcement operation known as Operation Restore Hope. UNITAF made great progress, and humanitarian agencies soon declared an end to the food emergency. By January 1993, food was getting to all areas of the country, and US forces began withdrawing in mid-February. On 4 May, UNOSOM II, armed with a much broader mandate that included nation-building activities, took over operations from UNITAF. With the benefit of hindsight, Colonel Kenneth Allard notes that at this point: "the

Somali militiamen man a .50 calibre M2 heavy machine gun in a truck converted for combat purposes. Estimates suggest there were up to 4,000 Somali fighters involved in the gun battle with UN forces.

underlying causes of conflict in Somalia had only been postponed", and it was during UNOSOM II that they resurfaced and "exploded".

The differences in scope between UNITAF and UNOSOM II were striking. While UNITAF focused on the southern parts of Somalia, UNOSOM II covered the entire country. While UNITAF strictly limited its activities to securing humanitarian assistance, UNOSOM II took on the much more dangerous task of disarmament. While UNITAF had no role in nation-building, UNOSOM II was mandated to assist Somalia in rehabilitating its political institutions, rebuilding its economy, and promoting national reconciliation and political settlement. Concerned with his "inability to get to US or UN forces in extremis", UNOSOM II deputy commander Major General Thomas Montgomery had requested armoured reinforcement, including a full mechanized battalion and an air cavalry squadron, in July 1993. Secretary of Defense Les Aspin denied the request, in Montgomery's mind "because the United States wanted out of Somalia, wanted to lower our troop presence, rather than increasing it."

OPERATION GOTHIC SERPENT

In its expanded mission, UNOSOM II directly threatened the Somali warlords

" ...in your tactics, avoid the enemy's strengths and attack his weaknesses... "

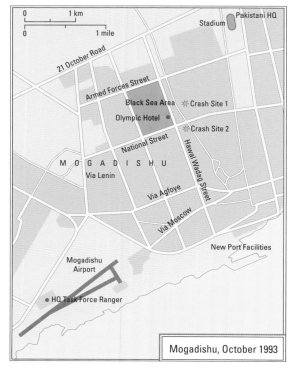

Mogadishu, October 1993

The easily blocked and difficult to navigate road network between the Mogadishu Airport and the crash sites presented numerous opportunities for ambush.

a suspected location of Aideed and his lieutenants at the Olympic Hotel. The Americans captured twenty of Aideed's men, but the mission quickly unravelled when Somalis shot down three US helicopters. The Americans soon became surrounded by thousands of Somalis, with some militiamen hiding behind unarmed women and firing from in between their legs and armpits.

The relief column was ambushed on its way to rescue the beleaguered soldiers, and it was more than nine hours before help, primarily from the 10th Mountain Division, finally arrived. Eighteen Americans were killed in the fighting.

The disaster had devastating effects on American support for a continued presence in Somalia. The Somalis displayed pictures of a dazed and bruised Chief Warrant Officer Michael Durant, the captured pilot of one of the downed Black Hawk helicopters. Somalis danced joyously amid the helicopter wreckage and dragged the beaten bodies of US soldiers through the streets. These images

in their quest for power. Major General Montgomery observes that, "[to build a nation] was not in the best interest of the warlords, who wanted, each of them, to control, and of course Aideed was the strongest of the warlords." What became the 3–4 October Battle of Mogadishu was part of a larger endeavour to capture Aideed known as Operation Gothic Serpent.

The operation had begun favourably, with a force of Army Rangers and Delta commandos conducting a daylight raid on

The stark contrast between a heavily armed and combat-ready American soldier and local Somalis sitting in the street indicates the confusing and fluid nature of the battlespace in Mogadishu.

invoked both outrage and shock in the American public. Although it is estimated that the Americans inflicted up to 2000 casualties on the Somalis during the Battle of Mogadishu, the American casualties and the chaotic nature of the operation created an outcry in the United States.

As a peripheral interest, Somalia had never evoked a deep US commitment, and the October fiasco led to the Clinton administration's decision to withdraw US troops by March 1994. The US withdrawal compelled the UN to terminate UNOSOM II and withdraw all peacekeepers by March 1995. Some observers, including Major General Montgomery, saw this development as the result of a calculated

strategy on behalf of Aideed. Walter Clarke, the deputy chief of mission at the US Embassy from March through July 1993 agreed, explaining, "I think he [Aideed] tended to look at the UNITAF period as a period of putting his force together, restoring some of his units, but certainly in preparation for events after UNITAF had gone… If he was going to get the UN out of there, which I think was clearly one of his objectives, he was going to have to take some actions." In Somalia, time was on the side of the belligerents rather than the peacekeepers; with their departure, Somalia quickly returned to the chaotic state in which it had been in mid-1992.

軍爭篇

孫子曰：凡用兵之法，將受命于君，合軍聚眾，交和而舍，莫難于軍爭。軍爭之難者，以迂為直，以患為利。故迂其途，而誘之以利，後人發，先人至，此知迂直之計者也。

軍爭篇

MANOEUVRES AGAINST THE ENEMY

❝ The stronger men will surge ahead and the weaker ones fall to the rear... ❞

I**N THE CONDUCT OF WAR**, the general receives his orders from the ruler; it is then the general's job to marshal the forces available to him, put them into effective order and build their encampment. Then, most difficult of all, he commences his manoeuvres against the enemy. The inherent difficulties of this lie in the need to turn the devious into the direct, and to turn the disadvantageous into advantage. For example, he may lay a false trail away from his true objective, so tempting the enemy off course, and thus arrive at his real destination before the enemy, even though he sets out after him.[19] This shows mastery of the devious.

---

[19] This rather cumbersome sentence, whose meaning does not really seem to justify its complexity, is an excellent example of the challenges of translation. In the original it is two carefully balanced three-character phrases of great simplicity which offer almost no clue as to their specific meaning.

故軍爭為利,軍爭為危。舉軍而爭利,則不及;委軍而爭利,則輜重 捐。是故卷甲而趨,日夜不處,倍道兼行,百里而爭利,則擒三將軍,勁者先,疲者後,其法十一而至;五十里而爭利,則蹶上將軍,其 法半至;三十里而爭利,則三分之二至。是故軍無輜重則亡,無糧食 則亡,無委積則亡。

故不知諸侯之謀者,不能豫交;不知山林、險阻、沮澤之形者,不能 行軍;不用鄉導者,不能得地利。

66 A ruler must understand the priorities of the local nobles before he can make profitable alliances... **99**

Manoeuvres against the enemy can bring great advantage or great peril. If you wait to muster your force with full equipment before trying to seize an advantage, you risk arriving too late. If you rush out under-equipped to seize an advantage, you risk also losing the equipment you left behind.[20] Equally to be considered is that if you order the men on forced marches with their armour rolled in their packs, moving night and day without rest to double the distance covered, then a march of 100 li to seize an advantage will result in the capture of the commanders of all three divisions. The stronger men will surge ahead and the weaker ones fall to the rear, and only a tenth of your strength will actually reach the destination on time. If the march is 50 li, then the leader of the vanguard will be captured, and half your force will arrive. If you march only 30 li, then two-thirds will arrive. On the same principles, an army must have its baggage train, provisions and supply dumps, otherwise it is lost.

A ruler must understand the priorities of the local nobles before he can make profitable alliances; a general must acquaint himself thoroughly with the terrain – its mountains and forests, its halts and impasses, swamps and marshes – before he can march his army through it. He must use local knowledge to take best advantage of the natural features.

---

[20] Commentators all agree that the text at this point is corrupt; this translation is the sense most usually adopted.

故兵以詐立，以利動，以分和為變者也。

故其疾如風，其徐如林，侵掠如火，不動如山，難知如陰，動如雷震。掠鄉分眾，廓地分守，懸權而動。先知迂直之計者勝，此軍爭之法也。

軍政曰：「言不相聞，故為金鼓；視而不見，故為旌旗。」夫 金鼓旌旗者，所以一人之耳目也；人既專一，則勇者不得獨進，怯者不得獨退，此用眾之法也。故夜戰多火鼓，晝戰多旌旗，所以變人之耳目也。

軍爭篇

66 **Victory belongs to him who has mastered the combination of the devious and the direct.99**

In warfare, subterfuge is your foundation, advantage your motivation, and circumstance determines your formation. You must be swift as the wind, dense as the forest, rapacious as fire, steadfast like a mountain, mysterious as night and mighty as thunder. Organize your men in the plundering of the enemy's country, allocate captured land amongst them to their best advantage, and do not act without careful consideration. Victory belongs to him who has mastered the combination of the devious and the direct. Such is the art of manoeuvring against the enemy.

The Book of Military Management[21] says: in battle, the human voice is not strong enough to be heard which is why we use gongs and drums; our eyesight is not acute enough, which is why we use banners and flags.

Gongs and drums, and banners and flags make the army hear with the same ear and see with the same eye. Thus unified in understanding, the brave cannot advance alone nor the cowardly retreat. This is the art of troop management. In night warfare, make more use of signal fires and drums, and in daytime rely on banners and flags, thus adapting to the eyes and ears of your troops.

---

[21] Stylistically, Sunzi's chapter ends with his formulaic sentence: "Such is the art of manoeuvring against the enemy." It is not clear why he then appends an extract from another book, nor is anything further known about this work. It is possible that the text has been corrupted by the inclusion into the text of what was originally a commentary or comparison by a later author.

故三軍可奪氣，將軍可奪心。是故朝氣銳，晝氣惰，暮氣歸。故善用 兵者，避其銳氣，擊其惰歸，此治氣者也。以治待亂，以靜待譁，此治心者也。以近待遠，以佚待勞，以飽待飢，此治力者也。無邀正正 之旗，無擊堂堂之陣，此治變者也。

故用兵之法，高陵勿向，背丘勿逆，佯北勿從，銳卒勿攻，餌兵勿食，歸師勿遏，圍師遺闕，窮寇勿迫，此用兵之法也。

> **66** ...do not get in the way of an army that is homeward bound... **99**

A whole army may become demoralized, and a general may lose heart. In the morning a soldier is full of fight, in the afternoon he is slowing down, and in the evening he thinks only of returning to camp. A skilled general will avoid the enemy when they are full of fight, and engage with them when their thoughts have turned to their beds. This is mastery of morale. He uses discipline in the face of disorder, and calmness to confront frenzy. This is mastery of emotion. To be close to the battlefield whilst the enemy is still far away, to be fresh and rested when the enemy is exhausted, to be well-fed when the enemy is hungry, this is mastery of the upper hand. Holding off from an enemy whose banners are well ordered, and not engaging with an army in tight formation, this is mastery of circumstance.

Here are some of the basic principles of war: never attack uphill, nor defend downhill; do not be lured into attack by feigned flight, and do not attack an enemy who is rested and full of fight. Do not swallow the bait put out for you, and do not get in the way of an army that is homeward bound. When you surround an enemy, always leave them a way out, and do not press a cornered foe too hard.[22] This is the art of waging war.

---

[22] These last three pieces of advice seem uncharacteristically soft on the enemy, but they should be understood not as letting the enemy get away, rather as denying them the savage courage that comes from desperation.

Mohi, 1241

Few armies have ever overcome an enemy so well in an open battle than the Mongols. And few of their battles demonstrate so well Sun Tzu's notion of a type of warfare that is mediated by knowledge and deception than the battle of Mohi in 1241. Also known as the battle of the Sajo River, this was a decisive event in the Mongol invasion of Europe.

The main consideration behind the Mongol incursion into Hungary was strategic: they believed that its flat grasslands would make an ideal grazing ground to act as a forward base for any future advance into Western Europe. In strategic terms, the mighty Danube River and its castles had the potential to act as a powerful natural barrier against any further incursion beyond Hungary. It was therefore unfortunate for the Hungarians that their rulers were incapable of putting up a united front that would match the challenge of their great river. King Bela IV faced opposition from rival barons; to make matters worse, the Hungarians were enticed away from the river and its numerous fortified settlements by the classic Mongol tactic of a false retreat. This was led by Batu, who enticed the Hungarian army away from Pest and the Danube towards open ground of the Mongols' own choosing.

SETTING UP THE BATTLEFIELD

The Mongols' chosen battlefield lay astride the small Sajo River, a tributary of the Tisza, which was crossed by a small stone bridge near the village of Mohi (Muhi). The Mongol army passed over the bridge and took up concealed positions some distance away, making camp on the rising ground separated from the river by swampy land. To frustrate any reconnaissance from the river side, they concealed their positions with brushwood. The ruse succeeded: when the Hungarians arrived, their scouts crossed the river and returned to report no sightings of the enemy. The Hungarian army therefore took up a position on the heath of Mohi, defended by a laager of chained wagons. They sensibly placed the river between them and the Mongols, but they pitched their tents rather too close together for safety, making the ropes holding them to the ground an obstacle to movement. Batu noted their ill-chosen camp, and likened them to cattle pent up in a narrow stable.

When night fell, Subadai led 30,000 Mongols further down the Sajo to prepare for a crossing that would take the Hungarians in the flank. Meanwhile, Batu and the main body began to engage King Bela across the stone bridge. Batu led a fierce attack on the bridge, which the

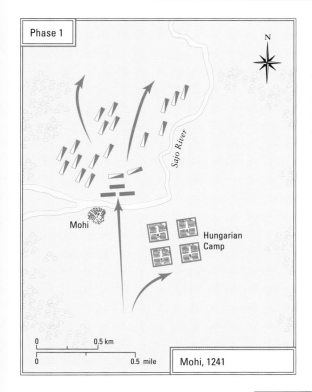

Mohi, 1241

In a night attack, the Hungarian forces (in blue) were initially able to seize the bridge at the River Sajo, destroying the Mongol vanguard in the process. The success gave them great confidence.

66 When you surround an enemy always leave them a way out... 99

The Mongols withdrew, sending a force to ford the river to the north. The next morning the Mongols attacked and regained the bridge. The main Mongol force was able to cross the bridge and attack the Hungarians. Having crossed the river to the north, the second force of Mongols joined the battle, surrounding the Hungarians in their camp.

Mohi, 1241

Hungarians had guarded with only 1000 men. Leading the defence of the crossing was King Bela's brother, King Coloman of the Ruthenians, who in the first onslaught hurled a Mongol officer, with his horse and weapons, off the bridge and into the river. Eventually, the hail of Mongol arrows and missiles forced him to return to camp, from where he returned with augmented forces. He fought until he and Archbishop Ugolin retired wounded, leaving a contingent of the Knights Templar still fighting. The Hungarian guards managed to hold the bank until the Mongols brought up catapults, with which they threw stones and fire bombs. With great determination, the Hungarian line held as their heavy cavalry absorbed the Mongol light horsemen's attacks and the missiles fell.

So resolute was the Hungarian defence that Batu began to have concerns about the likelihood of victory. He was encouraged only by the arrival of Subadai, who had forded the river upstream and surprised the Hungarians in the flank. Yet still the line held, so the Mongols stepped up the catapult bombardment until all the Hungarian tents and field fortifications were wrecked. The Mongols then prepared very conspicuously for a mass charge. Here, another example of

Sun Tzu's principles came into its own, because Subadai did not completely surround the camp. He realized that a cornered enemy will fight to the death, so he left an obvious escape route. At first, only a handful of horsemen took advantage of it, but once the panic spread, armour and weapons were discarded as a human flood began in the Hungarian camp, and all was confusion as the terrified knights tripped over the tent ropes in their eagerness to flee. Naturally, the hole in the Mongol lines led to ground of the Mongols' own choosing: the gap fed into a swamp. The Mongols calmly let the enemy run through their ranks, to be hunted down by the light cavalry afterwards, shooting down fugitives as if on a hunting expedition back in Mongolia. A chronicler later noted that the land was strewn with corpses for a two-day journey.

FURTHERING THE DECEPTION
Further psychological and deceptive warfare occurred soon afterwards when the Mongols took over the camp and found the great seal of the Hungarian chancellor. With it, they issued false proclamations in his name telling the inhabitants not to fear the Mongols but to stay in their houses. This ruse succeeded

66 A skilled general will avoid the enemy when they are full of fight... 99

as well, so there was no effective opposition to the Mongol advance nor any escape to fortified positions. Hungary was effectively abandoned. King Bela IV escaped from Mohi, as did his brother Coloman, who made it to his territories of Croatia and Dalmatia, only to die there of his wounds. When King Bela reached Pressburg (Bratislava) in safety to take refuge with Duke Frederick of Austria, the latter was contemptuous of the Hungarians' plight; he extracted a large ransom from the king before sending him on his way. It was a suitably ironic comment on a classic victory fought on sound ancient principles.

This 13th century manuscript illustration shows the Hungarian knights, many decked in great helms, fighting the Mongol cavalry on the bridge near Mohi.

九變篇

孫子曰：凡用兵之法，將受命于君，合軍聚眾，圮地無舍，衢地交和，絕地勿留，圍地則謀，死地則戰。

途有所不由，軍有所不擊，城有所不攻，地有所不爭，君命有所不受。

故將通于九變之利者，知用兵矣；將不通于九變之利，雖知地形，不能得地之利矣；治兵不知九變之術，雖知五利，不能得人之用矣。

九變篇

THE NINE VARIABLES [23]

" A general who thoroughly understands the Nine Variables will know how to use his armies. "

IN THE CONDUCT OF WAR, the general receives his orders from the ruler; it is then the general's job to marshal the forces available to him. If the terrain is unfavourable, do not encamp; if roads and communications are good, make sure of your allies; do not linger in difficult ground; if you are surrounded, find a way out by stratagem; in a life-or-death situation, fight head-on. There will be roads that should not be followed; there will be armies that should not be attacked; there will be cities that should not be besieged; there will be positions that should not be fought over; there will even be orders from your ruler that should not be followed. [24] A general who thoroughly understands the Nine Variables will know how to use his armies. A general who does not thoroughly understand them, however well he knows the lie of the land, will not be able to turn it to his advantage. A commander may be well acquainted with the Five Advantages, [25] but, without understanding of the Nine Variables, he will never use his men to their best effect.

---

[23] Sunzi does not in fact list nine variables. Some commentators suggest that "nine" simply means a very large number, which seems improbable on a number of counts. Given the shortness of the chapter, it is perhaps more likely that the text is corrupt and a portion is missing.

[24] This is Sunzi at his most pragmatic – and daring. In any circumstances apart from war, loyalty and obedience to your ruler should be paramount.

[25] Another argument for corruption of the text in this chapter since these are not defined, whereas a few lines later, the five pitfalls that may ensnare a general are carefully described.

是故智者之慮, 必雜于利害。雜于利, 而務可信也; 雜于害, 而患可 解也。

是故屈諸侯者以害, 役諸侯者以業, 趨諸侯者以利。

故用兵之法, 無恃其不來, 恃吾有以待也; 無恃其不攻, 恃吾有所不 可攻也。

故將有五危: 必死, 可殺也; 必生, 可虜也; 忿速, 可侮也; 廉潔, 可辱也; 愛民, 可煩也。凡此五者, 將之過也, 用兵之災也。覆軍殺將, 必以五危, 不可不察也。

九變篇

> **" ...reckless disregard for death will indeed result in death; too much regard for life will result in capture... "**

A wise leader always considers both advantages and disadvantages equally. By pausing to consider the disadvantages of an advantageous situation, he can be sure of achieving his aims; by considering the potential advantages of a perilous situation, he can find a way of resolving his difficulties. Keep the other lords and princes in their place by harrying them; worry them and keep them busy; lead them on with the hope of some advantage.

In waging war, do not rely on the enemy not arriving to battle but on your own readiness to receive them; do not rely on them not attacking, rather be sure of the defensibility of your own position.

There are five pitfalls that may ensnare a general: reckless disregard for death will indeed result in death; too much regard for life will result in capture; a quick temper can be provoked into rash action; a misplaced sense of honour brings only shame; over-solicitude for the men just causes needless trouble and anxiety. These five are the common failings of generals and are disastrous in their effect on the successful conduct of war. When an army is defeated and its general slain, look no further than these five for the cause. They demand study.

Mobei, 119 BCE

The Chinese Han Dynasty (206 BCE–220 CE) had been troubled with raids and invasions from the Xiongnu (known to the West as Huns) for many decades. As the Han Dynasty continued to strengthen during the reign of the Wu emperor, military expeditions were organized to deal with the threats from the north once and for all. The idea was to invade the Xiongnu homelands, in what could be described as one of the largest pre-emptive attacks in all of military history.

The preparations for these expeditions were lengthy and thorough. Chinese cavalry were improved both in quantity and quality to counter the famed mobility of the Xiongnu. Chinese infantry were equipped with a variety of weapons, to include crossbows (the Chinese being centuries ahead of Europe with this weapon). Well-built chariots, with trained drivers and horses, also augmented Han Dynasty forces.

THE CHALLENGE OF THE DESERT

The Xiongnu, anticipating possible Han offensives, withdrew their forces further northwards, putting much of the Gobi Desert between them and the Chinese. This did not dissuade the Wu Emperor: two separate invasion forces were sent against the Xiongnu, long distances across the desert notwithstanding. The words of Sun Tzu can be cited somewhat ironically here: "There will be roads that should not be followed; there will be armies that should not be attacked; there will be cities that should not be besieged; there will be positions that should not be fought over;

there will even be orders from your ruler that should not be followed." In the long term of the campaign, most of the Chinese losses would be due to the long distances and desert conditions. These losses would involve mostly the horses of the armies.

The Wu Emperor favoured one of his generals, Huo Qubing, and gave him an army of 100,000 infantry and 50,000 cavalry, including most of the elite troops available. The older general, Wei Qing, was given an army roughly as large, but containing far fewer elite troops. Wei Qing was also saddled with several ambitious subordinates. He was expected to use his experience to manage the egos of these generals. The most troublesome was the famous Li Guang, who, despite his reputation as one of the strongest and bravest of Chinese soldiers, had never achieved his lifelong ambition of being granted the title of marquis ("Huo" given as the Chinese equivalent).

Faulty intelligence led the Han to believe that the main Xiongnu forces were to the northeast. Therefore, under the notion of winning potentially greater

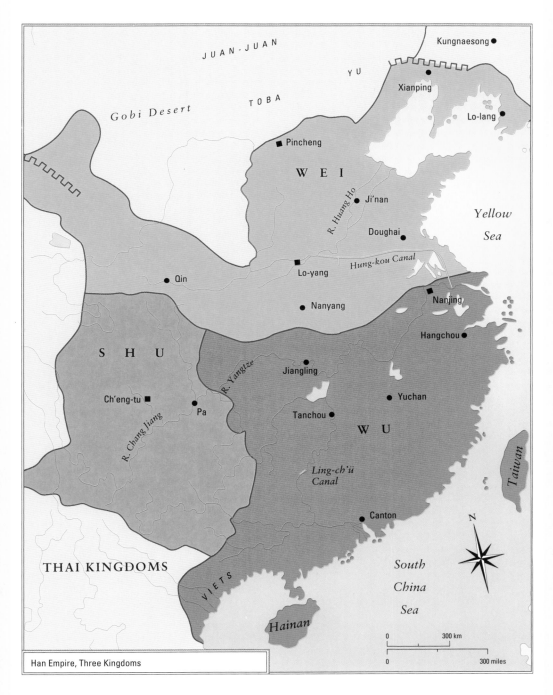

Han Empire, Three Kingdoms

In 119 BCE, the Han Dynasty sought to neutralise the threat from the northern barbarians by launching a strategic offensive into the Gobi Desert, to the north of Han lands.

66 In waging war, do not rely on the enemy not arriving to battle, but on your own readiness to receive them... 99

glory, Huo Qubing was directed to target those. Wei Qing was to target the supposedly weaker Xiongnu forces to the northwest. To arrange this allocation of forces, the two armies had to cross their routes and change directions.

As events proved, Huo Qubing ended up confronting the weaker Xiongnu force, and easily defeated them, inflicting losses of more than 70,000. His Han forces suffered half that number of losses in the fighting. Larger losses in horses were suffered, however, due to the 1610-km (1000-mile) march through desert lands, and then the pursuit of the Xiongnu, all the way to Lake Baikal. The result was the almost total annihilation of Xiongnu forces under their Worthy Prince of the East in the area.

Meanwhile, the Han force under Wei Qing marched 805km (500 miles) in the effort to track down the Xiongnu. Wei Qing had dispatched the relentlessly ambitious Li Guang with a large flanking force. Unfortunately, this detachment was lost in the desert when a huge Xiongnu army under Chanyu struck the Han army under Wei Qing's direct command. Wei Qing had his attached chariots form a defensive perimeter, with infantry and crossbowmen inside to resist the Xiongnu

onslaught. His cavalry he placed in reserve to protect the rear approach.

Wei Qing may have remembered Sun Tzu's words: "if you are surrounded, find a way out by stratagem; in a life-or-death situation, fight head-on". In any case, his quick thinking worked. The Han forces held firm, and dusk came with a sandstorm. Wei Qing exploited the storm by launching his cavalry in a counterattack on both flanks. The Xiongnu were repulsed with heavy losses.

When Li Guang and his detachment finally arrived, far too late for the battle, he was faced with an imminent court-martial. To avoid this, he committed suicide. As Sun Tzu observed, "a misplaced sense of honour brings only shame". Regardless, Wei Qing was able to pursue the routed Xiongnu, capture and burn a fortress, and return in triumph.

A PRE-EMPTIVE STRIKE

The overall campaign had crushed the Xiongnu and eliminated them as a threat to Han China for the foreseeable future. The objectives of the campaign had been achieved with total success. Losses to Han forces had been severe, especially in horses, with more than 110,000 of 140,000 horses with the armies perishing. Losses

A statue celebrating the Han general, Huo Qubing, stands today in Lanzhou, Gansu Province.

in men had been significant, with more than 20,000 cavalrymen dead, plus large but unknown numbers of infantry killed in action or dying from disease and exposure.

The objective had not been to conquer the Gobi, or the lands north of the Gobi, but rather to secure Han China against any further threat from the Xiongnu. The cost had been quite high, but the Han armies had returned essentially intact.

Sun Tzu says at the beginning of The Nine Variables that in the conduct of war the general receives his orders from the ruler, and then the rest is up to him. Both Huo Qubing and Wei Qing had done their duty, although the Wu Emperor was certainly fortunate to have such a resourceful veteran general in Wei Qing, even if he had not been the most favoured at the outset of the campaigns.

行軍篇

孫子曰：凡處軍、相敵，絕山依谷，視生處高，戰隆無登，此處山之 軍也。

絕水必遠水；客絕水而來，勿迎之于水內，令半濟而擊之，利；欲戰者，無附于水而迎客；視生處高，無迎水流，此處水上之軍也。

絕斥澤，惟亟去無留；若交軍于斥澤之中，必依水草，而背眾樹， 此處斥澤之軍也。

平陸處易，而右背高，前死後生，此處平陸之軍也。

行軍篇

ON THE MARCH

66 Never climb to join battle on high ground... 99

I N THE MATTER OF SITING YOUR OWN CAMP and observing the movements of the enemy, pass by the mountains and stay within the valleys, but choose an elevated spot for your camp facing east. Never climb to join battle on high ground. That is what you need to know about mountain terrain.

Once you have crossed a river, move well away from it. If the enemy crosses a river offering combat, never try to meet them mid-stream; you can seize the advantage by letting half their force across and then attacking. However eager you are for battle, do not attack the enemy as they approach a river; choose an elevated spot facing east to wait for them, and never attack upstream. This is how to fight around rivers.

Cross salt-marshes as quickly as possible and do not linger. If you come to battle in such marshes, fight in the water-meadows with trees at your back. This is how to fight in salt-marshes.

On level ground where it is easy to set up camp, choose a spot with high ground to your right and rear so that the danger is in front of you and safety behind. So much for fighting on level ground.

凡此四軍之利，黃帝之所以勝四帝也。

凡軍好高而惡下，貴陽而賤陰，養生而處實，軍無百疾，是謂必勝。

丘陵堤防，必處其陽，而右背之。此兵之利，地之助也。上雨，水沫至，欲涉者，待其定也。凡地有絕澗、天井、天牢、天羅、天陷、天隙，必亟去之，勿近也。吾遠之，敵近之；吾迎之，敵背之。軍旁有險阻、潢井、葭葦、林木、蘙薈者，必謹慎復索之，此伏奸之 所處也。

行軍篇

❝ All armies love the high ground and hate the low... ❞

It was through knowing how to use these four types of terrain to advantage that the Yellow Emperor was able to vanquish the Four Emperors.[26]

All armies love the high ground and hate the low, and prefer sunny places to dark and shade. If you look after the health of your men and camp on firm dry ground, your army will avoid all the usual diseases. This is a sure recipe for victory.

When you come to hills or man-made banks, take up position on the sunny side with the high ground to your right and rear. This will deploy your men to their best advantage, and make full use of the terrain. If a river is swollen with rain-water and you wish to cross it, wait until it subsides. If you encounter mountain cascades, deep hollows, dead ends, deep undergrowth, swamps or narrow ravines, keep well clear of them and stay away. At the same time try to force the enemy towards such places, so that you are facing them and they have them to their rear. If the army is passing through hilly ground where there may be ponds with reed beds or woods with thickets, these must be thoroughly searched for they are ideal cover for spies and traitors.

---

[26] The Yellow Emperor was one of the legendary rulers of Chinese mythological history, accepted as a real figure at this time. There is, however, no surviving story of him conquering four other emperors. We must presume it was lost over the centuries.

敵近而靜者，恃其險也；遠而挑戰者，欲人之進也；其所居易者，利也。

眾樹動者，來也；眾草多障者，疑也；鳥起者，伏也；獸駭者，覆也；塵高而銳者，車來也；卑而廣者，徒來也；散而條達者，樵采也；少而往來者，營軍也。

辭卑而備者，進也；辭強而進驅者，退也；輕車先出其側者，陣也.

行軍篇

If the enemy are close at hand but holding back from attack then they are confident in the strength of their position. If the enemy are far off but seem to be challenging you to battle, then they are trying to lure you in close. If their encampment seems open to attack, then it is a trap. If trees and bushes seem to be moving, the enemy is advancing. If you see unusual clumps among the reeds and grasses, the enemy is laying some kind of trap. If birds suddenly rise in their flight, there is an ambush[27] and startled animals mark a surprise attack. If dust rises high and distinct in the air, it is a sign of chariots; if the dust stays low but spreads out, it has been caused by infantry. When the dust separates along several different paths, the enemy are out collecting firewood. Small clouds of dust moving to and fro mean the enemy is pitching camp. If the enemy's heralds are conciliatory while the army still makes ready, then they are going to advance. If the heralds are haughty and the army looks ready to attack, they are preparing to retreat. If their chariots sally out and take up position on the flanks, the enemy is forming up for battle.

> **“ If trees and bushes seem to be moving, the enemy is advancing. ”**

---

[27] This does not mean birds rising from cover when disturbed by the enemy taking up position for an ambush. More subtly it means that birds in flight will deviate upwards from their course when flying over concealed men.

無約而請和者,謀也;奔走而陳兵者,期也;半進半退者,誘也。

杖而立者,飢也;汲而先飲者,渴也;見利而不進者,勞也;鳥集者,虛也;夜呼者,恐也;軍擾者,將不重也;旌旗動者,亂也;吏怒者,倦也;粟馬肉食,軍無懸缶而不返其舍者,窮寇也;諄諄翕翕,徐與人言者,失眾也.

數賞者,窘也;數罰者,困也;先暴而後畏其眾者,不精之至也;來委謝者,欲休息也。兵怒而相迎,久而不合,又不相去,必謹察之。

兵非貴益多也,惟無武進,足以并力、料敵、取人而已。

行軍篇

Offers of a truce with no solid commitments only indicate some kind of plot. If you see their troops rushing about and forming up, a decisive attack is coming. If the enemy seem to be half advancing and half retreating, it is a trap. If the soldiers are leaning on their spears, they are hungry; if those sent to draw water drink before they bring it back, the whole army is thirsty. If the enemy don't avail themselves of a clear opportunity, then they are exhausted. A place where birds gather undisturbed is unoccupied. Disturbance in camp at night means the enemy is fretful. Widespread unrest indicates weakness in the command. If the flags and banners begin to move around, there is disorder amongst the troops. If the officers seem angry and irritable, exhaustion is setting in. If the enemy are feeding grain to their horses and slaughtering their animals for meat, if they no longer hang up their cooking pots and return to their tents, then they are readying themselves for the final onslaught. Clusters of men whispering together are a sign of disaffection in the ranks.[28]

If rewards are being offered too freely, the enemy's resources are severely depleted. If punishment is being meted out too freely, the enemy is in dire straits. For the enemy general to start by being overbearing to his troops but end in fear of them is the height of stupidity. If their heralds come speaking soft and conciliatory words, they want a truce. If their troops come out in anger and form up opposite you for a long time without either engaging or retreating, be especially on your guard. If you hold no advantage in troop numbers, there is a military stalemate, and all you should do is concentrate your forces in one place, keep watch on the enemy and raise more troops.

---

[28] In this paragraph Sunzi shows himself to be not just a master of tactics but also of behavioural psychology.

夫惟無慮而 易敵者,必擒于人。卒未親附而罰之,則不服,不服則難用也。卒已親附而罰不行,則不 可用也。故令之以文,齊之以武,是謂必取。令素行以教其民,則民 服;令素不行以教其民,則民不服。令素行者,與眾相得也。

行軍篇

A general who recklessly underestimates the enemy is sure to be captured. A general who punishes his troops before he has won them over, will never be accepted by them and they will be useless to him. If he has already won them over but does not punish them when appropriate, they will still be useless. So you must bring your troops together with humane treatment, and bind them with discipline – this is the path to invincibility. Enact consistency in orders and instruction and the men will be loyal to you; if there is no consistency, they will not. It is of mutual benefit to general and men to maintain this consistency.

66 A general who punishes his troops before he has won them over, will never be accepted by them and they will be useless to him. 99

Jena–Auerstädt, 1806

In 1806, Napoleon made short work of the vaunted Prussian army, utterly defeating it in two battles fought on the same day: 14 October. The key to Napoleon's stunning victories at Jena and Auerstädt lay in his strategic deployment and the operational movement of his army.

The Prussian army performed well during the French Revolutionary Wars, leading to a negotiated peace with France in 1795. A decade later, during Napoleon's war with Austria and Russia, French troops violated Prussian territory; this led to hostility from Berlin. Napoleon soothed Prussian anger by offering them the captured territory of Hanover and a military alliance. Hanover was formerly a British royal possession. King Frederick William III agreed to the French terms, but months later Napoleon secretly offered Hanover to Britain in exchange for peace. The British informed the Prussians. Betrayed by their supposed ally, Prussia mobilized for war with France in September 1806.

NAPOLEON'S STRATEGY

Napoleon's *Grande Armée* was deployed in southern Germany. It was organized into six *corps d'armée*, each of two to three divisions commanded by a Marshal of France. In addition, the army included the Imperial Guard corps, a cavalry reserve and Bavarian allies. All told, the army fielded around 170,000 men. The Prussian army, with its Saxon allies, numbered 118,000 men.

Napoleon had excellent strategic intelligence but lacked solid operational knowledge of the enemy's movements and intentions. He therefore had to contend with an enemy whose plans were unknown. Napoleon took every precaution for the army's march, making sure that he would not be surprised by the Prussians to the north and northwest. He also needed to guard his right flank in case the Austrians intervened from the east. These strategic considerations resulted in the creation of what Napoleon termed *un battalion carré* (a "battalion-square").

Taking advantage of the extensive road network in Thuringia, Napoleon deployed his army into three columns that would march along parallel routes, connected by secondary roads over a 61-km (38-mile) front. The first column on the right consisted of two corps and the Bavarian army: 60,000 men. The centre column comprised two corps, the Imperial Guard and the cavalry reserve: 70,000 men. The left column of two corps totalled 40,000 men. Each corps was a half-day's march from the neighbouring corps, so that within 24 hours the army could be united on the battlefield. The columns were

Napoleon held the French Imperial Guard in reserve at Jena. It is reported that several soldiers shouted at the Emperor to send them into battle. Napoleon supposedly responded: "Let him wait until he has commanded in 30 pitched battles before he dares give me advice."

preceded by cavalry, whose job was to locate the Prussian army.

At the end of the first week of October, the Prussian army converged in the Saxon duchies, with an advanced guard of 8000 under Prince Louis Ferdinand. The army was divided into three groups: the main column of 50,000 men under the Duke of Brunswick and the king; the second under Prince Hohenlohe with 40,000 men; and General Rüchel's 20,000 Saxons. The Prussians marched south, seeking to engage the French in battle on the west bank of the Saale River, which protected their left flank. Napoleon,

however, marched north along the east bank of the Saale.

On 10 October, the Prussian advanced guard under Prince Louis Ferdinand clashed at Saalfeld with Marshal Jean Lannes' V Corps of the *Grande Armée* on the east bank of the Saale River. Prince Louis was killed and his troops dispersed. Napoleon and the Prussians had found each other. The Duke of Brunswick, commander of the Prussian army, was surprised by the French advance on his left flank. Napoleon, however, was quite pleased to learn of the location of the Prussian army and manoeuvred his corps

The defeat of Hohenlohe's army at Jena was so rapid that only a portion of the French army was engaged in combat. The dramatic victory was followed by an even more decisive pursuit of the fleeing Prussians by Marshal Murat's cavalry reserve corps.

rapidly along the east bank with the intention of conducting a *manoeuvre sur les derrières* (an encirclement). He ordered Marshal Bernadotte's I Corps to move north and cross the Saale at Dornberg, while Marshal Davout's III Corps would continue to Naumberg, and then west to cut the Prussian line of retreat. The rest of the army would converge on Jena, where Napoleon believed the main Prussian army was located.

TWO VICTORIES IN ONE DAY
When Brunswick realized his predicament, he ordered a withdrawal and concentration of the army, but it was too late. Prince Hohenlohe's forces

were already hounded to Jena, where he could be supported by Rüchel's troops to the west. Brunswick and the main army were camped 21km (13 miles) north, not far from Auerstädt. Hohenlohe misinterpreted the strength opposing him. He was skirmishing with only Lannes' single corps, whom he outnumbered. Instead of withdrawing upon the main army, he decided to engage Lannes on 14 October, and asked Rüchel for support. Now the genius of Napoleon's *battalion carré* became evident. By the morning of 14 October, Napoleon had concentrated 95,000 men at Jena – more than double Hohenlohe's army. The result was the complete destruction of Hohenlohe's and

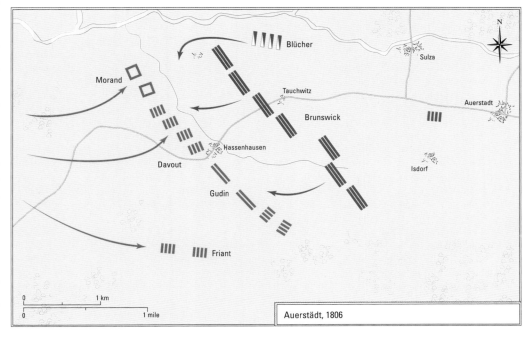

Auerstädt, 1806

Napoleon's *battalion carré* led to an overwhelming concentration of force on the field of Jena, but at Auerstädt, Marshal Davout's corps (in red) stumbled into the main Prussian army. Marshal Bernadotte's corps, 10km (six miles) to the south, was supposed to provide desperately needed support, but it never arrived.

Rüchel's forces at Jena by late afternoon. The Duke of Brunswick marched 21km (13 miles) northeast. To his surprise, the Prussian advanced guard under the indefatigable General Gebhard von Blucher encountered the lead division of Marshal Davout's III Corps. The Battle of Auerstädt, fought the same day as Jena, found the main Prussian army of 60,000 men under Brunswick fighting with Davout's 30,000 men. The battle was hard-fought, but the French troops held their ground and gradually manoeuvred around the Prussian right flank, cutting the route to Hohenlohe's army to the south. The Duke of Brunswick was mortally wounded during the battle, and the Prussian army withdrew from the field with heavy casualties.

The following day, Napoleon ordered his cavalry reserve to pursue the fleeing Prussians. Over the next weeks, tens of thousands of prisoners were taken and fortresses surrendered. The King of Prussia fled east and the French marched into Berlin in the third week of October.

The dual victories of Jena and Auerstädt on 14 October 1806 were the product of an experienced French army and the strategic and operational genius of Napoleon's *battalion carré*. His methodical deployment and march of the *Grande Armée* led to one of the most decisive military victories in history.

地形篇

孫子曰：地形有通者、有挂者、有支者、有隘者、有險者、有遠者。

我可以往，彼可以來，曰通。通形者，先居高陽，利糧道，以戰則利。可以往，難以返，曰挂。挂形者，敵無備，出而勝之，敵若有備，出而不勝，則難以返，不利。我出而不利，彼出而不利，曰支。支形者，敵雖利我，我無出也，引而去之，令敵半出而擊之，利。

地形篇

TERRAIN

❝ If neither side can gain the upper hand by taking the initiative, that is called neutral ground. ❞

TERRAIN MAY BE CLASSIFIED THUS: passable ground, entangling ground, neutral ground, narrow passes, rugged cliffs, and separating ground.

Passable ground is terrain that can be crossed by either side. To keep the upper hand in this kind of ground, make sure that it is you who occupy the sunny heights, and look to your supply lines. Entangling ground is such that although easy to sally forth from it is hard to re-occupy. On such ground, if the enemy is poorly prepared it is easy for you to venture out and defeat them. If, however, the enemy is well prepared and your attack fails, it will be difficult for you to return and you will be at a severe disadvantage. If neither side can gain the upper hand by taking the initiative, that is called neutral ground. In this kind of terrain, even though the enemy may offer me a tempting advantage, I would restrain myself and draw the enemy out. Then, when his army is half-committed, I would be able to attack with the certainty of gaining the upper hand.

隘形者，我先居之，必盈之以待敵。若敵先居之，盈而勿從，不盈而從之。險形者，我先居之，必居高陽以待敵；若敵先居之，引而去之，勿從也。遠形者，勢均，難以挑戰，戰而不利。凡此六者，地之道也，將 之至任，不可不察也。

故兵有走者、有馳者、有陷者、有崩者、有亂者、有北者。凡此六者，非天之災，將之過也。夫勢均，以一擊十，曰走。卒強吏弱，曰馳。吏強卒弱，曰陷。大吏怒而不服，遇敵懟而自戰，將不知其能，曰崩。將弱不嚴，教道不明，吏卒無常，陳兵縱橫，曰亂。將不能料敵，以少合眾，以弱擊強，兵無選鋒，曰北。凡此六者，敗之道也，將 之至任，不可不察也。

地形篇

66 Collapse occurs when the senior officers forget their responsibilities and take personal affront at the enemy. **99**

As for narrow passes, I make sure I occupy and fortify them first, then wait for the enemy to enter. If the enemy gets there first, and he has had a chance to fortify the position, then do not follow him in. If, however, the pass is unfortified, you should follow and attack. Amongst rugged cliffs, if I get there first, I occupy the sunny heights and wait for the enemy. If they get there first, I restrain myself and try to draw them out. If you are in separating ground, and the two sides are evenly matched, it is difficult to come to battle and even if you do, you will gain no advantage. These are the six principles of terrain and it is a prime responsibility of any general thoroughly to understand them.

There are six degrees of misfortune which can befall an army, none of which stem from natural causes but all of which are the fault of the general. They are: flight, insubordination, decline, collapse, chaos and rout. Flight results when, on otherwise equal terms, one force attempts to attack another ten times its size. Insubordination results when the rank and file soldiers are strong but the officers weak. If the officers are strong and over-bearing and the rank and file too passive, the result is decline. Collapse occurs when the senior officers forget their responsibilities and take personal affront at the enemy. They will then attack on their own account before the general has been able to assess the chances of success. If the general is weak and does not enforce discipline; if his orders are not clear; if there is no consistency for officers and men and organization is haphazard, all this results in chaos. When the general is unable to make an accurate assessment of the strength of the enemy, he will end up pitching a small detachment against a larger one, or a weak one against a strong one, without putting his crack troops in the vanguard. The result is rout. These are the six paths to defeat and it is a prime responsibility of any general thoroughly to understand them.

夫地形者,兵之助也。料敵制勝,計險厄遠近,上將之道也。知此而n用戰者必勝;不知此而用戰者必敗。故戰道必勝,主曰無戰,必戰可也;戰道不勝,主曰必戰,無戰可也。故進不求名,退不避罪,惟人是保,而利合于主,國之寶也。

視卒如嬰兒,故可以與之赴深谿;視卒如愛子,故可與之俱死。厚而 不能使,愛而不能令,亂而不能治,譬若驕子,不可用也。

地形篇

> **" If you treat your soldiers like your children, you can lead them into the deepest, darkest place. "**

The natural characteristics of the terrain are a soldier's friend. An ability to assess the enemy and control the chances of victory, to calculate obstacles, dangers and distances: these are what make a great general. If he understands all this and puts it into practice, he is certain of victory. If he neither understands nor practises it, he will be defeated. If all these indications point to certain victory, then a general must fight, even if his ruler orders him not to. Equally he must defy his ruler's order's to fight if the signs do not point to victory. A general who advances without thought of personal glory, and retreats without a care for disgrace, who thinks only of protecting the people and benefitting his ruler – such a man is a treasure beyond price to his country.

If you treat your soldiers like your children, you can lead them into the deepest, darkest places; if you see them as your beloved sons, they will stand by you to the death. If, however, you are too soft and do not establish firm leadership, too kindly and do not enforce your orders, if you are lax in your organization and cannot keep control – then your troops will be as useless to you as spoilt children.

知吾卒之可以擊，而不知敵之不可擊，勝之半也；知敵之可擊，而不 知吾卒之不可以擊，勝之半也；知敵之可擊，知吾卒之可以擊，而不 知地形之不可以戰，勝之半也。故知兵者，動而不迷，舉而不窮。故曰：知己知彼，勝乃不殆；知天知地，勝乃可全。

地形篇

These situations are only half-measures towards victory: knowing your own troops are prepared to attack, but not knowing the preparedness of the enemy; knowing the state of the enemy, but not of your own troops; knowing the readiness of both the enemy and your own troops, but not knowing the nature of the terrain. Thus also the experienced soldier only makes a move when he is sure of his direction and only takes to the road when he is sure of his supplies. This is why it is truly said: if you know the enemy and know yourself, you are sure of victory. If you know Heaven and Earth, your victory will be complete.

66 Thus also the experienced soldier only makes a move when he is sure of his direction and only takes to the road when he is sure of his supplies. 99

Gettysburg, 1863

The importance that Sun Tzu places on terrain is illustrated by the pivotal role that Little Round Top played on the second day of the Battle of Gettysburg, on 2 July 1863. As the day began, this critical point in the Federal line was undefended. General Gouverneur Warren, the Federal chief engineer, discovered this oversight and quickly initiated measures to correct it. In so doing, Warren demonstrated Sun Tzu's assertion that: "An ability to assess the enemy and control the chances of victory, to calculate obstacles, dangers and distances: these are what make a great general."

Cemetery Ridge stretched south of Gettysburg for some 3km (2 miles). At the north end of this low ridge was Cemetery Hill, rising about 24m (80ft) above Gettysburg. Baltimore Pike flowed into Cemetery Hill from the southeast. To the east of Cemetery Hill was Culp's Hill, about 30m (100ft) higher. At the south end of Culp's Hill was Spangler's Spring, a natural water source. The road to Taneytown ran parallel to the ridge on the east side. At the south end was Little Round Top and, below it, Big Round Top.

TAKING ADVANTAGE OF POSITION

The Federal line assumed the shape of a fishhook, with the tip being at Culp's Hill, the hook curving around Cemetery Ridge, and the eye at the two Round Tops. Although Big Round Top was the taller of the two hills, Little Round Top had been recently cleared of timber, and therefore offered better observation and fields of fire. Lee's men wrapped around the outside of the Federal "fishhook",

with Richard Ewell in the north, A.P. Hill in the centre and James Longstreet in the south. Such a configuration gave the Federal commander, George Meade, key advantages in terms of observation and fields of fire as well as central position. Moreover, the fence-enclosed fields, woods and orchards that lay in between the Round Tops and the Emmitsburg Road increased the difficulty of moving and controlling an attacking force.

Lee soon received confirmation from the reconnaissance he had sent to the south that the Federal line did not extend far in that direction. Only pickets occupied the southern portion of Cemetery Ridge, while the Rounds Tops were thus far unmanned. Lee initially wanted Ewell to attack Cemetery and Culp's Hills on the Federal right, but Ewell expressed reservations. Instead, Lee ordered Longstreet to make the main attack against the left of the Federal line in the vicinity of the Little and Big Round Tops. Longstreet would then turn north

It was military geography that transferred Gettysburg from a sleepy market town to a battlefield. All told, ten roads led to Gettysburg, making it a natural place to concentrate troops.

The Federal 1st Minnesota defend Cemetery Ridge, 2nd July 1863. Command and control limitations often necessitated densely packed formations in the Civil War and made manoeuvre through wooded areas difficult. Without cover and concealment, soldiers were subjected to devastating fire.

and roll up the enemy flank. Ewell and Hill would make secondary attacks in the north to prevent Meade from shifting forces to confront Longstreet in the south.

As Lee became increasingly impatient, Longstreet slowly made his preparations for the attack; it was noon before he began to move. Once he got started, Longstreet realized that if he continued on his planned route he would soon come under observation from the enemy. To avoid this danger, he was forced to order a countermarch and pick up an alternate route; this caused a two-hour delay. It was not until 3.30 p.m. that Longstreet's corps began moving into its attack position west of the Emmitsburg Road, with John Bell Hood's division on the right and Lafayette McLaws' on the left.

With the slow start and subsequent delays, the Confederate attack did not begin until 4.30 in the afternoon. By then, the Federals had had the opportunity to recover from a serious error in which Dan Sickles had failed to cover the key Little Round Top with his III Corps. The vulnerability was not discovered until

3 p.m., when Meade and his chief engineer, Gouverneur Warren, reconnoitred the III Corps lines.

Warren had an excellent understanding of the military value of terrain and the overall Federal situation. As he and Meade advanced, Warren pointed to Cemetery Ridge and noted, "Here is where our line should be." Meade only replied, "It is too late now." Still, Meade's trust in Warren was complete; he told him: "I wish you would ride over and if anything serious is going on, attend to it." With that, Warren rode off in the direction of Little Round Top.

A RUSH TO ACTION

From that vantage point, Warren could see the Confederates forming to attack the undefended Federal position. "The discovery," he wrote later, "was intensely thrilling to my feelings, and almost appalling." Realizing the urgency of the situation, Warren rushed into action, hurrying Strong Vincent and his brigade to the scene. Joshua Chamberlain's 20th Maine, the advanced regiment of Vincent's brigade, arrived only some ten minutes before Confederate William Oates and his 15th Alabama Regiment attacked his position.

Between Big and Little Round Top was a 460m (1500ft) saddle; as Oates descended into it, he did not see a single enemy soldier on Little Round Top. Along the way, he was joined by three more Confederate regiments that had manoeuvred around Devil's Den and the western base of Big Round Top. Now, as

Along the base of the two Round Tops, a small stream called Plum Run wound through broken ground. The Round Tops formed the eastern face of Plum Run Valley, and Houck's Run, the largest spur coming off Cemetery Ridge, formed most of the western face.

Large rock formations, such as these at Devil's Den, proved to be obstacles for advancing soldiers and cover for defending ones.

Oates began to climb up the southeastern slope of Little Round Top, he was met by "the most destructive fire I ever saw" from Chamberlain's newly arrived and well-covered Maine regiment less than 45m (150ft) to Oates' front.

Oates tried to get out of this devastating fire by working his way around the Federal left flank, but Chamberlain countered by dropping his left wing back to form a V-shaped position. The fighting became desperate. Chamberlain ordered his men to charge, personally leading them with his sword drawn. At nearly the same time, the Alabamians began receiving fire from their rear from the sharpshooters they had

66 Amongst rugged cliffs, if I get there first, I occupy the sunny heights and wait for the enemy. 99

fought through earlier. Oates had little choice but to abandon his attack.

The 20th Maine suffered 130 casualties in the fight, more than one-third of its 386-man strength. Such a great sacrifice was critical to the Federal cause. Had the Confederates been able to gain Little Round Top, they could have rolled up the Federal flank along Cemetery Ridge. In the actual fighting, Chamberlain saved the day for the Federals and won the Medal of Honor, but it was Warren's earlier realization of the importance of terrain that had made that outcome possible.

A Confederate soldier lies dead close to Little Round Top, one of the more than 4,000 men of Hood's Division who attempted to storm the high ground on 2nd July 1863.

九地篇

孫子曰:用兵之法,有散地,有輕地,有爭地,有交地,有衢地,有重地,有圮地,有圍地,有死地。諸侯自戰其地,為散地。入人之地 不深者,為輕地。我得則利,彼得亦利者,為爭地。我可以往,彼可以來者,為交地。諸侯之地三屬,先至而得天下眾者,為衢地。入人 之地深,背城邑多者,為重地。山林、險阻、沮澤,凡難行之道者,為圮地。所從由入者隘,所從歸者迂,彼寡可以擊我之眾者,為圍地。疾戰則存,不疾戰則亡者,為死地。

九地篇

THE NINE TYPES OF GROUND

❝ Territory that is of equal benefit to both sides is contentious ground. ❞

IN MILITARY TERMS there is dispersing ground, slight ground, contentious ground, open ground, linking ground, significant ground, difficult ground, constricted ground and desperate ground.[29] If a local ruler is fighting in his own territory, that is dispersing ground. If you have advanced only a short way into enemy territory, that is slight ground. Territory that is of equal benefit to both sides is contentious ground. If territory provides access and egress to both sides, it is open ground. Linking ground has borders with three different states, so that whoever controls it controls the bulk of the Empire. If you are deep in enemy territory, with many captured and garrisoned cities behind you, you are in significant ground. Forested mountains, rugged cliffs, marshes and wetlands – all territory that is hard to cross – is difficult ground. Territory with narrow access from which there is no direct retreat, so that a small force can easily defeat a large one, is called constricted ground. If you have to fight for your life and the least delay spells disaster, that is desperate ground.

---

[29] It has to be admitted that the translation of the names for each type of ground is fairly arbitrary since even in the original, the words take their meaning from their definitions rather than have a clear meaning in their own right. Other translators offer different versions, all equally acceptable.

是故散地則無戰,輕地則無止,爭地則無攻,衢地則合交,重地則掠,圮地則行,圍地則謀,死地則戰。所謂古之善用兵者,能使敵人前後不相及,眾寡不相恃,貴賤不相救,上下不相收,卒離而不集,兵合而不齊。合于利而動,不合于利而止。

敢問:"敵眾整而將來,待之若何?"曰:"先奪其所愛,則聽 矣。"

兵之情主速,乘人之不及,由不虞之道,攻其所不戒也。

九地篇

So, do not fight on dispersing ground and do not halt on slight ground. Do not attack on contentious ground and maintain your communications on open ground. Form alliances on linking ground and take the opportunity to plunder significant ground. Keep marching through difficult ground and use cunning when on constricted ground. On desperate ground, you fight. The great soldiers of old could separate the enemy's van from their rear, could prevent their small detachments and main force working together, stop the crack troops from helping the lesser divisions and disrupt communications between officers and subordinates. They could scatter the enemy and stop them from re-uniting, or keep them in confusion if they did manage to regroup. They would advance if it was advantageous or hold their position if it was not.

The question may be asked: what if the enemy advances to the attack with a large, well-organized army? My answer is: seize something they value highly, then they will listen to you.

The essence of military operations is speed. Take advantage of the enemy being unprepared; march by unexpected routes, and attack where they are not fortified against you.

66 ...march by unexpected routes, and attack where they are not fortified against you. 99

凡為客之道：深入則專，主人不克。掠于饒野，三軍足食。謹養而勿勞，并氣積力，運并計謀，為不可測。

投之無所往，死且不北。死焉不得，士人盡力。兵士甚陷則不懼，無所往則固，深入則拘，不得已則鬥。

是故其兵不修而戒，不求而得，不約而親，不令而信。

禁祥去疑，至死無所之。

九地篇

> **Do not be afraid to send your troops into a position from which there is no retreat...**

The principles for campaigning in enemy territory are as follows: the deeper you penetrate, the greater the feeling of solidarity amongst your own troops, making it even more difficult for the enemy to withstand them. If you find yourself in fertile terrain, then forage enough supplies for your whole army. Look to the well-being of your soldiers and do not over-work them. Keep up their spirits and conserve their energy. Unite your forces with ingenious tactics and keep the enemy off-balance.

Do not be afraid to send your troops into a position from which there is no retreat, for they will prefer death to flight. If they can look death in the face and not flinch, then there is nothing that will be beyond them: both officers and men will exert themselves to the utmost. Soldiers of whatever rank lose their fear in dangerous circumstances; they stand firm when there is no retreat; deep in hostile territory, they show a united front; when there is no alternative, they will fight to the last.

Such soldiers will always be on their guard without your prompting; they will achieve your goals without your having to ask; they will be loyal without inducement and can be trusted to act correctly even without orders.

Ban all omen-taking and superstitious practices so that death is all they have to worry about.

吾士無餘財，非惡貨也；無餘命，非惡壽也。令發之日，士卒坐者涕沾襟，偃臥者淚交頤。投之無所往者，諸、劌之勇也。

故善用兵者，譬如率然。率然者，常山之蛇也。擊其首則尾至，擊其尾則首至，擊其中則首尾俱至。敢問："兵可使如率然乎?"曰："可。"夫吳人與越人相惡也，當其同舟而濟，遇風，其相救也，如左右手。

是故方馬埋輪，未足恃也。齊勇如一，政之道也.

剛柔皆得，地之理也。
故善用兵者，攜手若使一人，不得已也。

<h1>九地篇</h1>

> **66** **Intelligent use of the terrain is the way to get the best out of both your strongest and your weakest men. 99**

Soldiers are not poor because they despise wealth, nor short-lived because they disdain long life. On the day of battle, their cheeks and their tunics will be wet with tears, but once they are at the point of no return, they will show the courage of Zhuan Zhu and the bravery of Cao Gui.[30]

The skilled soldier should follow the example of the Shuai-Ran[31] – the famous snake of Chang Shan: if you attack its head, it strikes with its tail; if you attack its tail, it strikes with its head; and if you attack its body, it strikes with both head and tail. You ask me if an army can imitate the Shuai-Ran? I say it can! Although the people of Wu and Yue hate each other, if two of them are in the same boat, caught in a storm, they will help each other just as the left hand helps the right.

You cannot rely merely on tethering the horses and burying chariot wheels to hold onto your troops; the way to manage them properly is to unite them in courage.

Intelligent use of the terrain is the way to get the best out of both your strongest and your weakest men.

The skilled general leads his troops by the hand as though they were a single soldier, and they cannot help but follow.

---

[30] In 515 BCE, Zhuan Zhu was employed by Prince Guang of Wu (later to become King He Lü) to assassinate the then ruler King Liao. He succeeded in doing so with a dagger concealed inside a fish, but was immediately himself killed. Cao Gui was a courtier of the state of Lu, which, in 661 BCE, was about to surrender a large portion of territory to the state of Qi after a series of defeats. As the Duke of Qi stood at the altar about to receive the surrender, Cao Gui seized him, held a knife to his throat and demanded that he return the territory to Lu. In fear of his life, the Duke agreed and Cao Gui calmly stepped back to his place among the other courtiers. The Duke's advisers told the Duke he could not lose face by reneging on this new agreement or by punishing Cao Gui.

[31] No-one has ventured a positive identification of this snake.

將軍之事：靜以幽，正以治。能愚士卒之耳目，使之無知。易其事，革其謀，使人無識。易其居，迂其途，使人不得慮。帥與之期，如登高而去其梯。帥與之深入諸侯之地，而發其機，焚舟破釜，若驅群羊。驅而往，驅而來，莫知所之。聚三軍之眾，投之于險，此謂將軍之事也。九地之變，屈伸之力，人情之理，不可不察也。

凡為客之道：深則專，淺則散。去國越境而師者，絕地也；四達者，衢地也；入深者，重地也；入淺者，輕地也；背固前隘者，圍地也；無所往者，死地也。

九地篇

It is the business of a general to keep tight-lipped to preserve secrecy; to be even-handed to ensure control; he must use tricks and rumours to keep both officers and men in the dark as to his true intentions. He should change his dispositions and plans, so no-one knows what he is up to. He should change his camp, and make detours so that his movements cannot be anticipated. When the time is ripe, a general should act like a man who climbs to a great height and then kicks away his ladder. He should plunge his army deep into enemy territory before he pulls the trigger. He is like a shepherd herding his flock to and fro so that no-one knows where he is really going. Marshalling his forces and leading them into danger is the business of a general. Adapting tactics to the Nine Types of Ground, assessing the merits of attack or retreat, understanding human nature – these are what demand a general's study.

When invading, the deeper you penetrate the better for holding your army together; if you stay too close to your own borders they will scatter. When you lead your troops across the border out of your own state, you are on difficult ground. If the terrain is accessible from all four directions, it is open ground. If you are deep into enemy territory, it is significant ground. If you are only a short way in, it is slight ground. If the enemy are entrenched behind you, and there are narrow passes ahead of you, it is constricted ground. When you have no way to turn, it is desperate ground.

66 It is the business of a general to keep tight-lipped to preserve secrecy... 99

是故散地，吾將一其志；輕地，吾將使之屬；爭地，吾將趨其後；交　地，吾將謹其守；衢地，吾將固其結；重地，吾將繼其食；圮地，吾　將進其途；圍地，吾將塞其闕；死地，吾將示之以不活。
故兵之情：圍則御，不得已則鬥，過則從。

是故不知諸侯之謀者，不能預交。不知山林、險阻、沮澤之形者，不　能行軍。不用鄉導，不能得地利。四五者，不知一，非霸、王之兵也。夫霸、王之兵，伐大國，則其眾不得聚；威加于敵，則其交不得合。是故不爭天下之交，不養天下之權，信己之私，威加于敵，則其城　可拔，其國可隳。施無法之賞，懸無政之令，犯三軍之眾，若使一人。犯之以事，勿告以言。犯之以利，勿告以害。

九地篇

❝ On desperate ground, I show my troops that the only choice left to them is between life and death. ❞

On dispersing ground, I bind my men with a common purpose. On slight ground, I keep my army in close formation. On contentious ground, I bring up my rearguard. On open ground, I look to my defences. On linking ground, I strengthen my alliances. On significant ground, I protect my supply chain. On difficult ground, I press forward on the route. On constricted ground, I block all the access points and exits. On desperate ground, I show my troops that the only choice left to them is between life and death. For, you must understand, it is the soldier's nature to fight back when surrounded, to struggle when he thinks all is lost, and to obey orders when in peril.

A leader must understand the priorities of the local nobles before he can make profitable alliances; he must acquaint himself thoroughly with the terrain – its mountains and forests, its halts and impasses, swamps and marshes – before he can march his army through it. He must use local knowledge to take best advantage of the natural features. If he does not understand even one of the basic principles of war, he is not a worthy general for his sovereign. A worthy general, when he attacks a powerful state, does not allow the enemy to concentrate his forces. He looms over them and prevents their allies from joining them. He does not strive to form alliances all over the place, nor does he look to bolster the power of other states. He keeps his own counsel, looming threateningly over the enemy. Thus he is able to capture their cities and conquer their kingdoms. Do not be bound by convention, but give rewards as they are merited, and issue orders according to the situation. Treat every man in your army exactly the same. Do not ask them simply to trust your word, show them with your actions. It serves no purpose to tell them if they are in danger.

投之亡地然後存,陷之死地然後生。夫眾陷于害,然後能為勝敗。

故為兵之事,在于佯順敵之意,并敵一向,千里殺將,是謂巧能成事 者也。

是故政舉之日,夷關折符,無通其使;勵于廊廟之上,以誅其事。敵人開闔,必亟入之,先其所愛,微與之期。踐墨隨敵,以決戰事。是 故始如處女,敵人開戶,後如脫兔,敵不及拒。

九地篇

66 If the enemy leaves you an opening, rush through it. 99

You can lead them into the most desperate of situations confident that they will survive, for victory is to be plucked from defeat when they are in the greatest danger.

In carrying out your military operations, give the appearance of being sucked into the enemy's plans whilst actually targeting their exposed flank. In this way even 1000 li won't save their general from your sword. This is how you use skill and cunning to achieve your aims.

On the day war is declared, close off the passes, cancel the command-tallies[32] and cease all communications with the enemy's ambassadors. Consider your plans carefully in the temple and make your preparations. If the enemy leaves you an opening, rush through it. Seize what they hold most dear, and constrain them as to time. Modify your plans according to the enemy's movements until you can bring him to the crucial battle. Start off as coy as a virgin until the enemy opens the door to you, then move with the speed of a hare so they have no chance to resist.

---

[32] Various forms of tallies – bronze animal figures, wood or bamboo tablets which could be split into matching halves – were used as symbols of rank and authority, as ways of confirming authenticity of orders and as passports.

Stalingrad,
June 1942–February 1943

The summer 1942 German offensive against the Soviets provides an excellent case study illustrating some of the "Nine Types of Ground" that Sun Tzu discussed. During spring 1942, the German Army in the East (*Ostheer*) planned an offensive through "significant ground" across the Eastern Front's southern sector during that summer. The offensive's objective was to capture the "contentious" ground of the northern Caucasian oilfields; securing the city of Stalin's name – Stalingrad – was a subsidiary aim.

The offensive comprised two stages: Axis forces would thrust east/ southeast to the Don River; these forces would advance on two separate axes, driving eastward to Stalingrad and southward into the Caucasus. With 1.4 million troops and 1495 AFVs, Army Group South commenced Operation Blue on 28 June 1942. The German Fourth Panzer, Second and Sixth Armies, plus the Hungarian Second Army, assaulted from the Kursk-Belgorod sector. These attacks aimed to drive east to capture Voronezh on the Don, thus sucking in the Soviet reserves. Once the Voronezh attack was underway, the rest of Army Group South (the German First Panzer and Seventeenth Armies, plus the Third Romanian Army), located further south in the Isyum-Taganrog sector, would join the offensive.

CROSSING OPEN GROUND
From 28 June to 6 July, the Second and Fourth Panzer Armies punched through the Soviet defences east of Kursk and pushed rapidly east to reach the Don at Voronezh across ground that was, in Sun Tzu's parlance, "open". With phase one completed, on 9 July Hitler divided Army Group South into Army Groups A and B. The latter was to clear the Donbass and then advance east to capture Stalingrad, while the former was to advance into the north Caucasian oilfields.

On 9 July, Fourth Panzer Army, at Voronezh, attacked southeast along the Don's western bank to link up with Sixth Army's eastward advance. That same day, the First Panzer, Seventeenth, and Third Romanian Armies struck from the Isyum-Taganrog area and advanced east/ southeast towards Rostov and the Don estuary to link up with Fourth Panzer Army. From 16 to 31 July, however, Hitler pointlessly diverted Fourth Panzer Army away from Stalingrad only to redirect it back there. Consequently, with the German Sixth Army remaining too weak to capture Stalingrad by itself in late July, the Soviets used this time to assemble a

German infantry manhandle a 7.5cm le.IG 18 infantry gun during the fighting for Stalingrad. The Germans quickly became bogged down in protracted urban warfare amidst "constricted" terrain.

powerful defensive force around the city's "constricted" and "difficult" terrain.

On 23 July, Hitler issued audacious new instructions: Army Groups A and B were respectively to secure the Baku oilfields on the Caspian coast and capture Stalingrad. On 25 July, Army Group A commenced its thrust south across the Don estuary into the northern Caucasus and by early August was advancing rapidly south across this "open" terrain in the face of modest enemy resistance. By 12 August, its forces had pushed 360km (224 miles) beyond Rostov to capture the Maikop oilfields and reach the Caucasus mountains. During

late August, however, the German advance into the Caucasus petered out, hampered by an over-extended logistical chain and Hitler's diversion of forces to the siege of Stalingrad.

SUCKED INTO STALINGRAD
During August and September, the psychological triumph of capturing Stalingrad grew powerfully in Hitler's mind; this obsession sucked Axis forces into a constricted area around the city, while in the Caucasus overstretched formations operated over vast frontages. Hitler had sensibly assumed that the Soviets would

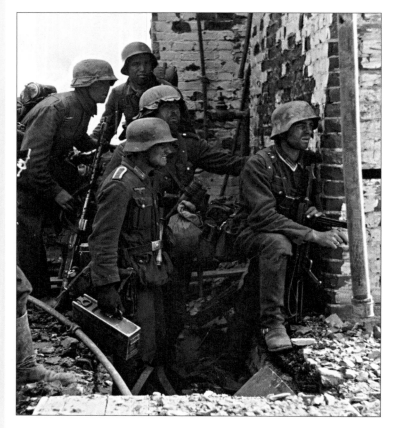

Elements of a German infantry section take shelter behind a ruined house in preparation for mounting an assault on the enemy's positions. The ruins of Stalingrad proved "decisive" terrain in the war on the Eastern Front.

resist fanatically to protect Stalingrad, enabling the Germans to surround and destroy them; this applied Sun Tzu's dictum that attackers should "seize something [the enemy] values highly".

The city was ground that in Sun Tzu's terminology was not only "difficult" and "contentious" but was also "decisive" terrain where the enemy would "fight to the death". But the battle panned out differently, with the Germans sucked into an intense urban battle within the city itself.

In September, the German Sixth and Fourth Panzer Armies fought their way forward metre by metre through the city's ruined streets, against fanatical Soviet resistance, toward the Volga River. This savage combat aptly reflected Sun Tzu's description of "desperate ground" where troops looked "death in the face and [did] not flinch". By allowing themselves to be ensnared in a protracted urban battle at Stalingrad, however, the Germans both played to the Red Army's strengths and failed to utilize effectively their superior operational mobility.

By 26 September, the Axis forces had fought their way forward until they reached the Volga River in the south of the city. By 18 November, after a further seven weeks of brutal urban fighting, the Axis forces had driven the Soviets back until the latter held a shallow 12-km-wide (8-mile) bridgehead adjacent to the Volga's western bank. Unbeknown

Soviet infantry make a defensive stand in a wrecked building somewhere in the city's factory district. The 62nd Army fought with its back to the river, reflecting the Red Army's determination to fight for "desperate ground" without counting the cost.

to the Axis, the Soviets had fed into Stalingrad just enough troops to prevent the Axis from capturing the city. The Soviet defence planned to draw in, fix, and then denude the Axis forces locked in this bitter "desperate" battle for the city; meanwhile, the Red Army was establishing the foundations for a devastating surprise riposte.

THE SOVIET COUNTEROFFENSIVE

By 18 November, the Germans believed that they were just a few days away from completing the capture of Stalingrad. This was proven wrong the next day when the Red Army initiated a surprise counteroffensive: Operation "Uranus". Throughout the "desperate" 11-week struggle for the city, the Soviets had

amassed powerful reserves – 50 divisions with 1000 AFVs – behind the Stalingrad sector. As planned, "Uranus" was ironically a simple German-style double envelopment that pitted Soviet strength against Axis weakness; namely, the overstretched Axis formations deployed across the northwestern and southern approaches to the city.

On 19 November, two powerful Soviet offensives smashed through these thin Axis defensive positions. Within five days, the Soviet spearheads had advanced 128km (80 miles) westward to meet up at Kalach, thus forming a shallow encirclement that netted the 220,000 troops of German Sixth Army deployed at Stalingrad. Stalin's city, moreover, remained "desperate ground" – except

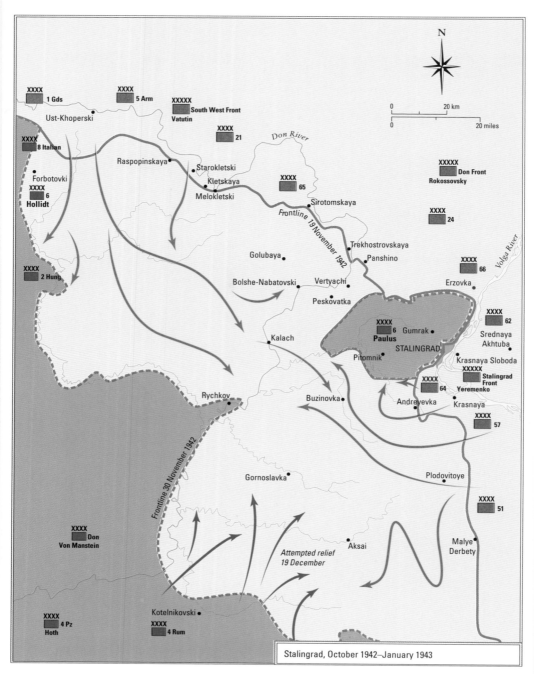

Stalingrad, October 1942–January 1943

In Operation "Uranus" the Soviets attacked the weakly held Axis fronts to the northwest and south of the German Sixth Army "fixed" in the bitter struggle for Stalingrad. Within five days the two Soviet envelopments had met up at Kalach, surrounding some 220,000 Axis troops.

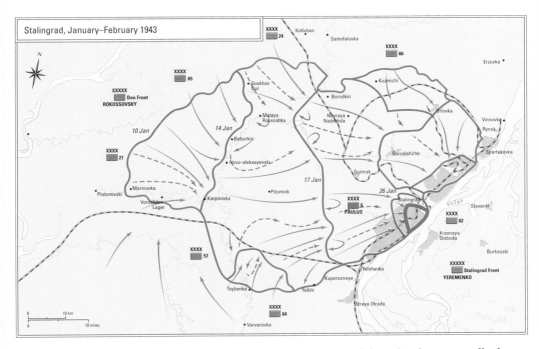

In early 1943, Soviet assaults drove the encircled Axis forces back into the city; eventually these attacks fragmented the pocket into three enclaves, before the inevitable capitulation occurred.

now it was the Axis troops who were fighting for their lives.

After being surrounded, the Sixth Army's only sensible option was to break out westward while German relief forces from outside the pocket broke back in. Hitler, instead, directed that the city must not be abandoned under any circumstances. Rather, Sixth Army was to form a defensive hedgehog while Axis troops outside of the pocket launched an offensive towards the city. In the meantime, the Luftwaffe was to resupply the Sixth Army by air with all the supplies it needed to maintain its combat power.

Unfortunately, intense Soviet countermeasures ensured that Sixth Army received only a fraction of the supplies it required. By 23 December, the German relief offensives towards the city had been thwarted by Soviet resistance. Meanwhile, the ever-weakening Sixth Army was subjected to repeated Red Army onslaughts as the latter reduced the size of the pocket and eventually split it into three enclaves. Finally, from 29 January to 2 February 1943, the remaining 91,000 German troops in Stalingrad, virtually out of food, munitions and fuel, capitulated.

The protracted intense battle for the "desperate ground" of Stalingrad has gone down in history as one of the most desperate and bitter battles of modern times.

火攻篇

孫子曰：凡火攻有五：一曰火人，二曰火積，三曰火輜，四曰火庫，五曰火隊。

行火必有因，煙火必素具。發火有時，起火有日。時者，天之燥也。日者，月在箕、壁、翼、軫也。凡此四宿者，風起之日也。

火攻篇

ATTACKING WITH FIRE

66 A general who attacks with fire is demonstrating his intelligence... 99

THERE ARE FIVE WAYS of attacking the enemy with fire. The first is to burn the troops themselves; the second is to burn their stores; the third is to burn their equipment; the fourth to burn their arsenals, and the fifth to use fire arrows.

You need specific materials to make a fire attack, and these should be prepared in advance. There are also an appropriate season and appropriate days for raising such an attack. The proper season is when the weather is dry, and the suitable days are when the Moon is in the constellations of the Sieve, the Wing, the Wall or the Cross-bar. These are all days when the wind will blow.

凡火攻，必因五火之變而應之。火發于內，則早應之于外。火發而其　兵靜者，待而勿攻。極其火力，可從而從之，不可從而止。火可發于　外，無待于內，以時發之。火發上風，無攻下風。畫風久，夜風止。凡軍必知有五火之變，以數守之。

故以火佐攻者明，以水佐攻者強。水可以絕，不可以奪。

火攻篇

"If it is possible, set fires towards the enemy from outside their camp..."

When mounting a fire attack, you must be prepared for five eventualities. If fire breaks out in the enemy's camp, be ready to make a swift attack. If however fire has broken out but the enemy are not panicked by it, then hold off your attack. Wait until the conflagration is at its height, take a view on whether it is practical to attack or not and act accordingly. If it is possible, set fires towards the enemy from outside their camp, don't wait to try to start fires inside, but seize the opportunity outside.

Remember to position yourself upwind of the fire you start, and never attack downwind of a fire. A wind that has blown for a long time during the day is likely to drop at night. Any army should be familiar with the five eventualities of a fire attack, and be prepared accordingly.

A general who attacks with fire is demonstrating his intelligence; one who uses water is simply showing his strength. Water can cut off an enemy, but it cannot despoil him of his equipment and supplies.[33]

---

[33] The inclusion of this brief comment on the use of water is puzzling in its lack of any detail or explanation. It is hard to see why Sunzi includes it as it adds nothing to the overall treatise. It may be supposed that the opportunities for serious attack using water were few and far between, and so there was little need to discuss them.

夫戰勝攻取，而不修其功者凶，命曰"費留"。故曰：明主慮之，良將修之。非利不動，非得不用，非危不戰。主不可以怒而興師，將不可以慍而致戰。合于利而動，不合于利而止。怒可以復喜，慍可以復悅，亡國不可以復存，死者不可以復生。故明君慎之，良將警之。此安國全軍之道也。

火攻篇

It is disastrous not to consolidate your achievements if you are victorious in battle and successful in your attacks – this is called waste and delay. Hence it is truly said that a wise ruler thinks ahead, and a good general builds on his victories. Do not move unless you see a clear advantage. Do not use your soldiers unless there is something to be gained. Do not fight if you are not in danger. A ruler should not call his general to arms simply out of anger; a general should not attack because he has been insulted. Only advance if it is to your clear advantage, otherwise stay put. Anger may change to contentment and insult to pleasure, but a kingdom once destroyed cannot be recovered, and the dead cannot be brought back to life. Thus a wise ruler is cautious, and a good general alert. This is the way to keep a country at peace and its armies intact.

66 ...a wise ruler thinks ahead, and a good general builds on his victories. 99

Ia Drang, 1965

Sun Tzu's instructions for attacking with fire can be interpreted as an explanation for the use of weapons generally and their applicability in specific environments. As the United States struggled to apply the full weight of its firepower in the jungles of Vietnam, it turned to the helicopter. The Battle of Ia Drang in 1965 became the pioneering effort to use the new air assault capability to defeat the communist forces.

The military strategy for American forces under the command of General William Westmoreland during the Vietnam War revolved around "search and destroy" operations. These battalion-size and larger operations were designed to "find, fix, flush, and finish" the enemy in a way that maximized traditional American reliance on the offensive: mass, firepower and technology. Westmoreland envisioned that using these operations would cripple the enemy's main force units and break the hold the communists exerted on the countryside. After these conditions had been established, Westmoreland reasoned, the South Vietnamese could accomplish pacification.

THE IMPORTANCE OF HELICOPTERS
Critical to search and destroy operations, and therefore perhaps the piece of equipment most associated with the Vietnam War, was the helicopter. Helicopters had seen limited logistical service in the Korean War, and in January 1963 the Army began forming and testing the 11th Air Assault Division to experiment with expanding helicopters into an active combat role.

The test program quickly gained momentum, and in September the Army conducted an exercise called Air Assault I that tested an airmobile battalion at Fort Stewart, Georgia. The results were promising enough to warrant further testing. By January 1964, the Army was actively contemplating the inclusion of an airmobile division in its force structure.

On 11 February 1964, the 11th Air Assault Division was formally activated at Fort Benning, Georgia, for the purpose of expanding the test program. After the successful completion of Air Assault II, Secretary of Defense McNamara authorized the organization of the 1st Cavalry Division (Airmobile) on 15 July 1965. The division began deploying to Vietnam in a matter of weeks.

The first combat test of the new airmobile concept, and the first major clash of the American and North Vietnamese armies, was fought in the Ia Drang valley of the Central Highlands shortly after the 1st Cavalry Division arrived in Vietnam. The stage for this

Introduced in the 1950s, the air assault concept used helicopters to transport soldiers to
battlefield combat rather than merely in logistical support roles. Here a UH-1D helicopter
departs the area after discharging a load of infantrymen during the Battle of Ia Drang.

battle was set when a PAVN army corps attacked a US Special Forces camp near Plei Me, not far from the Cambodian border. The North Vietnamese strategy was to lure a South Vietnamese relief column to rush to the aid of the besieged Americans and then ambush the South Vietnamese. Instead, the United States and the South Vietnamese launched a massive counterattack involving ground units, artillery and tactical air support to defeat both the force attacking Plei Me and the force trying to ambush the relief column. The PAVN then withdrew to their Cambodian sanctuary after suffering an estimated 850 killed and 1700 wounded.

❝ Do not use your soldiers unless there is something to be gained. ❞

Helicopter transportation reduced, but certainly did not eliminate, the necessity of ground movement by foot. Here members of the 1st Cavalry march through rugged terrain en route to Chu Phong mountain in the Ia Drang Valley.

SEARCH AND DESTROY

Hoping to follow up on this initial success, Westmoreland called on the 1st Cavalry to launch a search and destroy operation. From 28 October to 14 November, the division conducted a series of air and ground searches in the Ia Drang valley. This would previously have been a nearly impossible task. The division's tactical area of operations covered over 2330 square kilometres (900 square miles), but extensive communications and helicopter mobility now allowed a single brigade to sweep a sector that large. Furthermore, helicopter mobility precluded the requirement for maintaining a central reserve. Once a battle started, every unit not in contact could be airlifted to the scene. The airmobile concept was changing the way the US Army fought.

For four days, the division's searches yielded no results. Then, on 1 November, 1st Cavalry soldiers found a map on a dead North Vietnamese officer showing unit locations and the routes designated for both the 32nd and 33rd NVA Regiments. This intelligence allowed the division to focus its search, and enemy contacts increased until a decisive battle was joined on 14 November. On that day, the 1st Battalion, 7th Cavalry Regiment, commanded by Lieutenant Colonel Harold Moore, began landing in a small clearing known as Landing Zone (LZ) X-Ray. Nearby were the 66th and 33rd NVA Regiments, which immediately began

66 It is disastrous not to consolidate your achievements of you are victorious in battle... 99

descending on the LZ. Shortly after noon, the Americans and North Vietnamese were in mortal combat.

As the embattled cavalrymen defended the landing zone, more than 8000 artillery rounds, Air Force fighter-bombers, and even B-52s flown in from Guam pounded the North Vietnamese. Despite intense fire on the LZ, reinforcements were flown in as well. Having attacked prematurely, the North Vietnamese committed their forces piecemeal and the Americans were able to shift from one threatened position to another to hold on.

The battle continued for two days; in the end, American tenacity and firepower carried the day. In the fighting at LZ X-Ray and nearby LZ Albany, the North Vietnamese suffered an estimated 3000 killed compared to 300 American losses. As the defeated North Vietnamese withdrew towards Cambodia, five battalions of South Vietnamese paratroopers flew to intercept them. Supported by American artillery, the South Vietnamese soldiers were able to inflict additional casualties before the North Vietnamese units made it across the border to safety.

Ia Drang confirmed in Westmoreland's mind the validity of the search and destroy concept and became the harbinger of more and larger such operations.

Helicopter mobility allowed the Americans to move an entire brigade into battle just hours after alert, whereas the less mobile North Vietnamese required weeks to plan and execute their efforts to achieve mass. However, while demonstrating the capabilities of an airmobile force, the Ia Drang campaign also indicated the difficulty in encircling and destroying the entire enemy – a problem that would plague future search and destroy efforts.

In addition, after suffering heavy losses at Ia Drang, the North Vietnamese merely reverted to guerrilla warfare, a move that largely negated the Americans' ability to create the conditions that had given them the advantage at Ia Drang. Finally, in another thematic problem, by the early summer of 1966, sizeable enemy units were returning to the Central Highlands and threatening the Special Forces camp at Plei Me.

Search and destroy operations that ultimately abandoned the battlefield allowed the North Vietnamese to return to it after the Americans had departed. Unless forces remained to secure the area, the whole process became a vicious cycle, proving Sun Tzu's prediction that: "it is disastrous not to consolidate your achievements if you are victorious in battle and successful in your attack."

用間篇

孫子曰：凡興師十萬，出征千里，百姓之費，公家之奉，日費千金。內外騷動，怠于道路，不得操事者，七十萬家。

相守數年，以爭一日之勝，而愛爵祿百金，不知敵之情者，不仁之至也。非人之將也，非主之佐也，非勝之主也。故明君賢將，所以動而勝人，成功出于眾者，先知也。先知者，不可取于鬼神，不可象于事，不可驗于度。必取于人，知敵之情者也。

用間篇

USING SPIES[34]

> **[Foreknowledge] can be obtained from men who have accurate knowledge of the enemy's situations.**

W HEN YOU LEVY an army 100,000 strong and set out on a campaign of 1000 li, the combined cost to the people and the public exchequer will be 1000 jin per day. There will be widespread disruption at home and abroad, people will fall exhausted at the roadside and as many as 700,000 families will be unable to do their daily work.

Spending years in stalemated campaigning, which could be settled in one day's decisive battle, because you are too miserly to lay out 1000 silver pieces in rewards to discover the enemy's circumstances: this is inhumane in the extreme. It is not the behaviour of a leader of the people, nor of a true prop to the ruler or a master of victory. For what enables a wise ruler and an able general to attack decisively and to succeed where ordinary men fail, is foreknowledge. And foreknowledge cannot be found by consulting the spirits, or by comparing similar situations. It is not to be found by measuring the movements of Heaven and the Earth; it can be obtained from men who have accurate knowledge of the enemy's situation.

---

[34] Sunzi's understanding of the necessity of an effective intelligence network, its efficient organization and the various levels of expendability of its agents is chillingly calculating...and modern.

故用間有五：有因間，有內間，有反間，有死間，有生間。五間俱起，莫知其道，是謂神紀，人君之寶也。

因間者，因其鄉人而用之。內間者，因其官人而用之。反間者，因其敵間而用之。死間者，為誑事于外，令吾聞知之，而傳于敵間也。生間者，反報也。

故三軍之事，莫親于間，賞莫厚于間，事莫密于間。非聖智不能用間，非仁義不能使間，非微妙不能得間之實。微哉！微哉！無所不用間也。

用間篇

To this end there are five types of spy you may use: the local spy, the internal spy, the converted spy, the expendable spy and the permanent spy. If you use all five types, no-one can fathom their machinations – it is a kind of divine organization, and is a ruler's greatest treasure.

Local spies are recruited from the enemy's peasantry, and internal spies from their court officials. Converted spies mean using the enemy's own spies against them. Expendable spies are those who are fed false information so that it may be picked up by the enemy's own spies. Permanent spies are the ones who concentrate on bringing back reports.

Thus in your whole army, none should be closer to you than your spies; none should be more richly rewarded; and no secret more closely guarded than your spy network. Spies must be used sagaciously and treated with benevolence and virtue; and you must use the utmost subtlety to be sure of obtaining true reports from your spies. Subtlety is the key! There are no circumstances where spies cannot be used.

❝ Expendable spies are those who are fed false information so that it may be picked up by the enemy's own spies. ❞

間事未發,而先聞者,間與所告者兼死。

凡軍之所欲擊,城之所欲攻,人之所欲殺,必先知其守將、左右、謁者、門者、舍人之姓名,令吾間必索知之。

必索敵人之間來間我者,因而利之,導而舍之,故反間可得而用也。因是而知之,故鄉間、內間可得而使也;因是而知之,故死間為誑事可使告敵;因是而知之,故生間可使如期。五間之事,君必知之,知之必在于反間,故反間不可不厚也。昔殷之興也,伊摯在夏;周之興也,呂牙在殷。

故惟明君賢將能以上智為間者,必成大功。此兵之要,三軍之所恃而動也。

用間篇

> **A wise ruler or an able general must select only the most intelligent men to act as his spies...**

If a spy lets slip information before a plan has come to fruition, then both the spy and anyone he has told must be put to death. Whether you wish to destroy an army, attack a city or assassinate somebody, the first essential is to identify by name the general in command, his attendants, his aides, his gatekeepers and bodyguards. You should order your spies to obtain this information.

When you find the enemy's agents spying on you, offer them bribes, lavish care on them and lodge them handsomely. Thus they may become converted spies and be of use to you. It is through these converted spies that you will be able to recruit local spies and internal spies. It is through them that your expendable spies will feed false reports to the enemy. And it is also through them that your permanent spies will be able to act as occasion demands. A ruler must know how to employ all five kinds of spy, and this understanding comes necessarily from the converted spy. Therefore treat none more generously than your converted spies. In ancient times, the rise of the Yin was due to the work of Yi Zhi, formerly in the employ of the Xia; and the rise of the Zhou was due to the work of Lu Ya,[35] formerly in the employ of the Yin.

A wise ruler or an able general must select only the most intelligent men to act as his spies and then he will be sure of achieving great things. This is a necessity of war, and an army depends on it to act.

---

[35] The Yin is an alternative name for the Shang Dynasty (c1500–1050 BCE), the second Bronze Age Dynasty which overthrew the original Xia (c2000–c1500 BCE). Yi Zhi, also known as Yi Yin, was a Xia statesman instrumental in its downfall who took high office under the Shang. Similarly, Lu Ya who helped overthrow the Shang and then served under the succeeding Zhou Dynasty (1050–770 BCE).

Shimabara, 1638

By 1600, Japan had known only a time of war for 150 years. The triumph of the Tokugawa family at the Battle of Sekigahara in October of that year promised a welcome peace. Indeed, only one serious outbreak of armed strife would occur during the subsequent two centuries of Tokugawa rule.

This outbreak happened in 1638 on the Shimabara peninsula in Kyushu, where what began as a peasant farmers' protest developed into a full-scale revolt again their local lord. The fanatical and desperate insurgents, most of whom were persecuted Christians, fortified themselves in the dilapidated castle of Hara on the Shimabara peninsula, from where they defied all attempts to defeat them. Eventually, the Shogun was forced to mount a full-scale expeditionary force from Edo, but what was expected to be a pushover turned into a long and bitter siege in which the use of spies by the Tokugawa was to prove crucial.

The conclusion of the siege of Hara owed much to the intelligent application of knowledge gained about the enemy; all this information came about through the use of spies. Out of Sun Tzu's five types of spy, we see no sign at Shimabara of expendable spies or those who could act as double agents among the rebel commanders. There was no time for the latter to have done their work. Instead, Hara Castle was infiltrated night after night by Sun Tzu's "permanent spies", who were specialists in the service of General Hosokawa Tadatoshi (1586–1641), the lord of Kumamoto.

THE INVISIBLE ONES

The intelligence-gathering operations were carried out by men referred to as *shinobi*, a word that means "the invisible ones". This is the original form of the expression commonly read nowadays as "ninja", the mysterious black-clad infiltrators whose exaggerated exploits are constantly retold in movies and comics.

The Hosokawa records present a dispassionate and disinterested account of real espionage carried out by genuine *shinobi*. They may well have dressed in black for camouflage at night time, but it is interesting to note how narrow is the definition of a *shinobi* skill in the Hosokawa material. Digging a hole under the wall to provide entry to the castle is not a *shinobi* operation, even though it provides some exciting reading, with the defenders thrusting spears down into the gap to flush out infiltrators. The word "shinobi" is applied only to intelligence gathering carried out through entering a castle in secret by climbing its walls, not by tunnelling beneath them.

According to the Hosokawa archives, the first night raid was carried out by *shinobi* under the command of Hirano Jibuzaemon in order to obtain a general

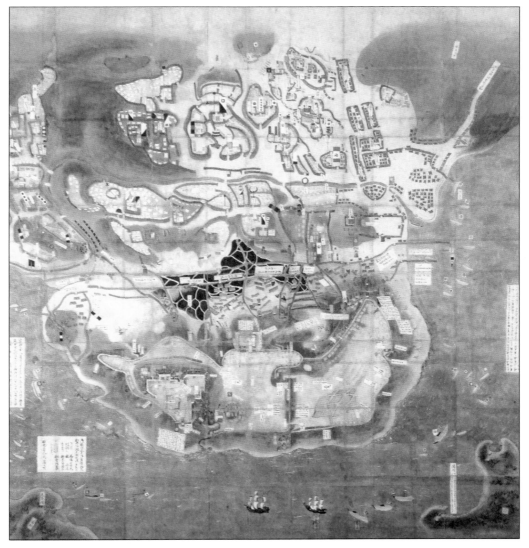

This 17th century painting shows the Siege of Hara Castle. The Tokugawa army occupies the land to the north, while two Dutch ships lie offshore ready to bombard the castle.

idea of the layout of the castle. They were ordered to reconnoitre the plan of construction of Hara, and to measure the distance from the defensive moat to the inner bailey. They were also ordered to estimate the depth of the moat, to assess the conditions of roads, the height of the wall, and the shape of the loopholes through which men could possibly climb.

A very noisy diversion was provided by Hosokawa's musketeers, who fired a volley into the open sky as the *shinobi* departed from the siege lines. This had the additional advantage of permitting

the *shinobi* to approach under the cover of darkness: as soon as the guns erupted, the defenders immediately doused all the lights, which were customarily provided from pine torches around the perimeter and within the castle. The garrison sentries were on full alert, but the spies concealed themselves in some brushwood and waited until the defenders relaxed their guard later in the night.

One of the Hosokawa *shinobi* infiltrated deep into Hara Castle, but was unable to glean much information because he was unfamiliar with the local dialect and the use of Christian expressions. His presence also aroused the defenders' suspicions, but the man escaped in a hail of stones. He took with him a Christian flag as proof of his actions, for which exploit he was awarded five silver coins on his return.

The following night, another individual, who is described as a *shinobi* under the command of Yoshida Suke'emon, returned from a raid with some severed rebel heads. However, finding that he was being pursued by fourteen or fifteen men, he discarded all but one of his trophies. There are no records of the information he brought back.

A few days later, two *shinobi* sneaked into the castle in a very unusual manner: they had ropes attached to them so that if they were shot they could be pulled back; but they returned successfully with useful information.

THE SUCCESSES OF SPIES

The historical account tells us that the Hosokawa had in total ten *shinobi* within their ranks and that they were used night after night. The information they brought back built up a vital dossier for the attacking forces ready for the important decision about when to launch a major assault, because every attempt over the previous few months had been beaten back and the defenders appeared to be as strong and as united as ever.

One *shinobi*, Uehara Heinosuke, heard the striking of a bell as he entered the castle on his spying mission. Realizing that it meant that the guard was being changed, he concealed himself. Another spy was not so fortunate and fell into a hole in the darkness, but this particular raid succeeded in capturing thirteen bags of provisions on which the enemy depended as an emergency lifeline.

The spies also obtained secret passwords that could be useful for confusing the garrison in a subsequent raid. However, the most important information that the *shinobi* brought back was the revelation that the garrison's food supplies were now

This 19th century woodcut shows a *shinobi* about to attack Prince Mitsuuji as he plays the *koto*. *Shinobi* were used for spying, not assassination in feudal Japan, but the image of the silent man in black has survived to this day.

almost exhausted. Patient observation by the *shinobi* at dawn had revealed that the defenders were reduced to eating the seaweed they were able to scrape off the rocks at low tide. Furnished with this crucial information, the Tokugawa commanders launched a massive attack and found that the defenders' strength was much reduced, just as the spies had indicated. The garrison of Hara nevertheless fought to the last man, with women and children wielding pots and pans in defence as the castle fell.

The fall of Hara Castle was to have far-reaching consequences for Japan. It had been a considerable embarrassment to the Tokugawa to have been frustrated by Christian peasants for so long. As Christianity was seen as an alien foreign import, the ultimate result was the seclusion of Japan from the Western world for the next two centuries.

Contributors

Ralph Ashby, a Gulf War veteran, earned his PhD from University of Illinois at Chicago in 2003. He has taught for Eastern Illinois University and DePaul University. His publications include *Napoleon Against Great Odds* (2010) and contributions to *The Encyclopedia of Warfare* (2013).

Miles Doleac is an Assistant Professor of Classics and Film at the University of Southern Mississippi. He is also a filmmaker, theatre director and actor, and author of *In the Footsteps of Alexander* (2014). He lives in Hattiesburg, MS, with his wife, Lindsay, and their five dogs.

Kevin Dougherty is the Assistant Commandant for Leadership Programs and an adjunct professor at The Citadel. He is a retired lieutenant colonel from the U.S. Army and has a doctoral degree in international development. He has written 15 books and numerous articles on a variety of military topics, including the Mexican War, the U.S. Civil War, World War II, the Vietnam War and various support and stability operations.

Stephen Hart is a senior lecturer at the Department of War Studies, the Royal Military Academy Sandhurst. He has written many books on military history topics, including *The German Soldier in World War II*, *Road to Falaise* and *Military Atlas of Tank Warfare.*

Frederick C. Schneid is Herman and Louise Smith Professor of History and Chair of the Department of History at High Point University in North Carolina. He is a European military historian who specializes in 18th and 19th century French and Italian military history. He is the author and editor of 16 books and has published numerous chapters and articles.

Stephen Turnbull is Visiting Professor of Japanese Studies at Akita International University in Japan. Now retired, he is an honorary lecturer at SOAS specialising in Japanese religion. He also writes about the military history of Japan and East Asia, with an additional strong interest in Eastern Europe.

Index